IMAGES
of America

GARRETT
FREIGHTLINES

This group photograph shows the members of the sales and management teams of Garrett Freightlines in 1952. It was staged in the boardroom of the new, state-of-the-art company headquarters building that had been completed only the year before. Clarence Garrett, the company's president and cofounder, is seated at the table at far left. (Courtesy of the Lawrence Allsberry Estate Collection.)

ON THE COVER: This promotional photograph from the late 1950s shows a Garrett Freightlines truck and trailer looking south toward the Portneuf Gap, the "Gateway to the Rocky Mountains," in Pocatello, Idaho. The image shows off the rugged beauty of Pocatello, at the time a town of nearly 30,000 people, one of the largest cities in Idaho and the home of Garrett Freightlines' headquarters for nearly seven decades. (Courtesy of the Steve Port Collection.)

IMAGES
of America

GARRETT FREIGHTLINES

Idaho State University's
"Management 4499/5599" Honors Class

Lisa Cecil, Michael Cellan, Doug Chambers, Jodi Diaz, Andrea
Jardine, Chelsea Kavanaugh, Jenna Larson, Melissa Myers, Somelina
Obiechina, Travis Pattengale, Brooke Rammell, Evette Reay, Daniel
Spicer, McKenzie Thomas, Lauren Wagner, and Jordan Withers

ARCADIA
PUBLISHING

Published by Arcadia Publishing
Charleston, South Carolina

Library of Congress Control Number: 2015956390

For all general information, please contact Arcadia Publishing:
Telephone 843-853-2070
Fax 843-853-0044
E-mail sales@arcadiapublishing.com
For customer service and orders:
Toll-Free 1-888-313-2665

Visit us on the Internet at www.arcadiapublishing.com

*To Ron and Patty Bolinger for their generosity and encouragement,
and to Lawrence and Bertha Allsberry, who inspired this book.*

CONTENTS

Acknowledgments

The authors—Lisa Cecil, Michael Cellan, Doug Chambers, Jodi Diaz, Andrea Jardine, Chelsea Kavanaugh, Jenna Larson, Melissa Myers, Somelina Obiechina, Travis Pattengale, Brooke Rammell, Evette Reay, Daniel Spicer, McKenzie Thomas, Lauren Wagner, and Jordan Withers—wish to thank Dr. Tom Ottaway, Michele O'Brien-Rose, and the College of Business Leadership Board at Idaho State University. Thank you to Mark Arstein, Debra Gerber, Susan Hooks, Heidi Wadsworth, John Ney, and Karma Morrison for encouragement and great ideas. We also wish to thank Dr. Kandi Turley-Ames and the College of Arts & Letters, and Dr. Kevin Marsh of the Department of History. Many thanks to Dr. Sherri Dienstfrey-Swanson and Dr. Jamie Romine-Gabardi of the University Honors Program, as well as Dr. Ellen Ryan of Special Collections at Oboler Library, who gave up many (most!) of her Monday nights to open Special Collections for our research. We also thank Gail Hunt for organizing the end-of-semester celebration (a "book signing before the books").

Thank you to the many individuals who donated the photographs, stories, and documents that formed the basis of this book. Rich Kirkham, the current owner of the Garrett Freightlines terminal building, hosted our class on a two-hour tour of the entire complex and loaned us photographs and documents. Thanks go to Ken Clements and the *Idaho State Journal* and Ryan Port and David Faust, who graciously allowed us to access their extensive collections of historic photographs. Thanks also to Tyler Cantrell for the aerial photographs.

Thank you to the former Garrett employees our class interviewed, including Terry Jensen, Darrell Scott, Spike Bunnell, Mary Brownley, Kirsten Serpa, Luanne Hemingway, Bob and Jeanne Pierce, and many people who shared with us their stories about Garrett Freightlines, including Sally Thompson, Jerry Tydeman, Bob Kalenda, Bob Garrett, the Covert family, the Schank family, Jerry Skaggs, Ray Lowe, Marilyn Davis, Jim Chapman, Bill Ryan, Lowell Nelson, Rex Waldron, and Bob and Kathy Phelps.

Thank you to Chris Gabettas in Marketing and Publicity at Idaho State University for helping to publicize this class and our activities, as well as Kyle Birdsell for help with advertising and logistics. Special thanks go out to our editors, Sarah Gottlieb, Jeff Ruetsche, Mike Kinsella, and Emilia Monell at Arcadia Publishing, for their help and support. Thank you to Dr. Alex Bolinger's parents, Ron and Patty Bolinger, his siblings, Elizabeth, Mark, and Jeff, and his uncles and aunts, Stan and Celeste Allsberry and Greg and Karla Allsberry, for advice and help.

To those not named here who supported this project in ways big and small, direct and indirect, we thank you—this book would not have been possible without you.

INTRODUCTION

The backstory about how this book came to be is almost as unique and unlikely as the story of Garrett Freightlines itself. My grandfather Larry Allsberry was my inspiration for this project. He spent his entire career at Garrett Freightlines and worked his way from a line driver to the president of the company. My grandparents left behind boxes of documents, photographs, and memorabilia from my grandfather's four decades with the company, and I have long had the feeling that I was sitting on a story of historical significance and human interest that should someday be told, but I wasn't quite sure how.

The moment of insight for how to bring this story to life came during a visit to the Ford Piquette Plant in Detroit, Michigan, where the original Model T vehicles were designed and produced. The handsome (if drafty) brick building reminded me, in vintage and character, of the original Garrett terminal on South First Avenue in the historic warehouse district of Pocatello. I also had a chance to tour Henry Ford's drafting room, where he and his engineers would brainstorm ideas for improving vehicle designs. At that moment, I was struck by the importance of creative teams brainstorming design innovations as a catalyst for the rise of the transportation industry in the United States.

I drafted a proposal for a class that would meet two goals. The first goal was to research and write about the history of Garrett Freightlines, one of the great entrepreneurial success stories in Idaho in the 20th century. The second goal was to provide a hands-on, real-life opportunity for students to grasp the challenges of working in teams on a creative project. We talked extensively throughout the semester about Pixar Animation (per Ed Catmull's recent best-selling book, *Creativity, Inc.*) as an exemplar of managing the tensions of collaborative creativity, such as building a climate where individuals feel safe and invested enough to speak candidly and to be held accountable for their contributions.

Putting the class together took the cooperation of many entities, and I am very grateful for the willingness of so many people to take a chance to support this endeavor. The History of Garrett Freightlines class at Idaho State University was a collaboration among the College of Business, the College of Arts & Letters, the Honors Program, and the Special Collections department at Oboler Library. My mom, Patty Bolinger, and her brothers, Stan and Greg Allsberry, willingly loaned the source materials from the Larry Allsberry Estate Collection that became the backbone of this book. Idaho State's Marketing and Publicity department enthusiastically supported and publicized this project from the outset. Rich Kirkham, the current owner of the Garrett Freightlines terminal building, opened his doors and generously led our class on a two-hour tour of the entire facility.

The *Idaho State Journal* in Pocatello not only allowed us to use historic photographs but also provided free advertising to encourage others from the community to donate their photographs to the cause. Ryan Port and David Faust allowed us to borrow hundreds of photographs related to Garrett Freightlines from their extensive collections. Arcadia Publishing took a risk by signing on to a project with not one, or a few, but 16 student authors. And those 16 students, in turn, signed up for a class that had never been offered before. This entire project has been an act of faith for everyone involved, and I cannot thank them enough for their openness to taking on the challenge.

Taking on a project as ambitious as asking a class to write a book in one semester requires outside support and encouragement. My parents, Ron and Patty Bolinger, believed in this idea from the beginning and provided financial backing and invaluable encouragement. It has been a long path from idea to reality, and with this book, our class has crossed the finish line. I hope you find this pictorial history of Garrett Freightlines to be interesting, thought-provoking, and perhaps even inspiring.

—Alex Bolinger
Assistant Professor of Management
Idaho State University, Pocatello

In structuring the story of Garrett Freightlines, our class faced a dilemma. On the one hand, the story proceeds in chronological order. There are distinct eras that move from the heady early days in 1913, when the company steadily grew from a single mechanized truck delivering freight and luggage around town into an intercity and interstate freight carrier, to the concluding decade following the death of the company's founder, when the success of Garrett Freightlines made it attractive to rivals with designs on a hostile takeover. Almost every era of Garrett's history brought new challenges, distinct characters, new innovations to the transportation industry, and growing financial and operational success. Chapters one (Clarence Garrett and the Early Years), six (Takeover Attempts and Labor Movements), and seven (The Fall and Legacy of Garrett Freightlines) focus more on the chronological.

On the other hand, much of the richness of the story of Garrett Freightlines has to do with the equipment, innovations, and day-to-day interactions that transcend eras and form the heart of what the company was and how it is remembered by its employees. Chapters two (Organizational Culture and Garrett's People), three (Trucks and Equipment), four (Terminals), and 5 (Safety) step outside the timeline to look in depth at the people of Garrett Freightlines, their activities at work and outside of work, and the plants and equipment that they used to serve customers throughout the western United States. We hope you enjoy this history of Garrett Freightlines in pictures.

One

CLARENCE GARRETT AND THE EARLY YEARS

The story of Pocatello's origins is deeply connected to transportation. In 1872, the Utah & Northern Railroad extended narrow-gauge tracks from Salt Lake City, through Portneuf Canyon, to Montana. By 1882, tracks were laid from Omaha to Portland, crossing the Utah & Northern Line at present-day Pocatello. This location assured Pocatello a future as a transportation center in the Intermountain West. The "Pocatello Junction" was a mere 40 acres with a collection of tents and boxcars to house construction crews.

In 1889, with a population of only 3,000, the commissioner of Bingham County declared the Village of Pocatello duly incorporated. This village status was maintained until 1893, when the Idaho state legislature formally recognized Pocatello as a city with a population of 4,000. By 1913, Pocatello had more than doubled in size to over 9,000 people. In this same year, on July 8, Clarence Garrett launched Garrett Transfer Company.

Early Pocatello was shaped by the "steel highway" (that is, the railroad). The city received its name in memory of an Indian chief and sits at the entrance of the Portneuf Canyon, which is why people refer to it as the "Gate City." What is now the second largest city in Idaho owes its humble beginnings and rapid growth to the railroad. The image below depicts the earliest days of old town Pocatello. Some of the buildings that would have seen upon entering the city in 1915 are the book store, the pharmacy, and the iconic Monarch Hotel. (Both, courtesy of the Historic Photographs Collection, Special Collections, Eli M. Oboler Library, Idaho State University.)

Founding of Multi-Million Dollar Business Began With 50c Drayage Fee

There are times when a meagre 25c can mean a great deal.

In this case it meant the founding of an $8 million business. Here's how it came about.

Back in August, 1909, Clarence A. (for Anson) Garrett, an ambitious lad of 19, decided to strike out for the building West where great opportunities beckoned. He bid his father farewell, packed his few beingings, and the drayman hauled his baggage to the station in the little town of Bristol, Va. The drayage charge was 25c.

Arriving at Pocatello, the young man had the drayman haul his baggage to the hotel. The charge was 50c.

"A horse and wagon at both ends, but here it costs 25c more for the same service," young Garrett said to himself. "This looks like a business where I might compete successfully and make a little more than wages."

As head of the vast Garrett Freightlines, Inc., with an annual volume of upward of $8,000,000, he's made considerably more "than wages." But it didn't come the easy way.

Anyway, he started in the drayage business. A year or so later, while he was visiting in Bristol, his father bought a small truck for his mercantile business. Clarence was impressed with the great potential of this mechanized manner of hauling.

Upon his return to Pocatello, he got together with his brother, Oscar, and cousin, Leonard and among the three of them they managed to scrape up $300. They purchased a 1913 Reo truck for $525, borrowing the balance from the First Security bank, and started hauling baggage.

It was a typical early-day truck hard rubber tires, kerosene lamps and springboard seat. Nevertheless, it beat a horse and wagon and it was capable of delivering groceries about the city and hauling trunks to and from the depot. A similar truck can be seen above the gatehouse of the new plant.

From this humble beginning, and with the realization there was great need for something new and bigger in transportation, Clarence worked hard to achieve his goal.

By gradually building an organization around his vision and progressive outlook the company expanded steadily through the years. The first line-haul operation performed by Garrett's was between Pocatello and Idaho Falls, 51 miles distant. The round trip required approximately 18 hours of jolting along on hard rubber tires through mud and sand.

In 1950, Garrett's huge fleet of 653 pieces of equipment covered 17,000,000 miles in seven western states.

A friendly, but quietly unas-

CLARENCE A. GARRETT
Real pioneer in trucking industry.

In 1909, Clarence Garrett headed west to Pocatello, the Gate City to the Rocky Mountains, at the age of 19. Having observed the growth of the city and the railroad, he recognized a unique opportunity to grow his business. Back in Virginia, Garrett noted that the draymen who transported luggage from railroad stations to their customers' destinations were charging much less than the draymen in Pocatello. It was this realization that led to a unique niche for his business. By 1951, the *Idaho Standard Journal* stated that Garrett Freightlines was an $8-million business. (Courtesy of the Lawrence Allsberry Estate Collection.)

This is among the earliest known photographs of the first vehicle in the Garrett fleet, a 1913 Reo purchased from Ransom E. Olds in Lansing, Michigan. Clarence Garrett, his brother, Oscar, and his cousin, Leonard, saved their money to purchase the vehicle, including chain drive, hard-rubber tires, a small bed for hauling goods, and kerosene lamps, for a total of $525. On the first day of operation, July 8, 1913, the Garrett brothers used the Reo to earn $4 for their first day's work. (Courtesy of the Stedtfeld Family Papers, Special Collections, Eli M. Oboler Library, Idaho State University.)

During World War I, Clarence Garrett was not drafted into the US Army, and the nascent Garrett Transfer Company was able to capitalize on the increased demand for transporting wartime supplies. Following the end of the war, Garrett Freightlines built on the demand from the war and continued to experience steady growth. (Courtesy of the Lawrence Allsberry Estate Collection.)

As Garrett Freightlines expanded and traveled all over the western United States, the company's main headquarters remained in Pocatello. There were calls from time to time to move the headquarters to a more populated, centralized area, but Clarence Garrett was loyal to Pocatello. Here, an early Garrett truck is parked in front of a stately building in old town Pocatello. (Courtesy of the Lawrence Allsberry Estate Collection.)

The original company headquarters were not located on the northwest end of the city but squarely in the heart of the commercial warehouse district. This photograph shows the company's first operating terminal building, located on South First Avenue east of the railroad tracks that bisected the city. (Courtesy of the Lawrence Allsberry Estate Collection.)

In addition to the cargo service Garrett Freightlines offered during the early years, the company also performed other unique services. During baseball season, Garrett Freightlines transported teams throughout the Yellowstone Circuit, hauling both players and cargo for Pocatello's team from city to city. The trucks never sat for long, because they also transported the fans of Pocatello to and from the games for 25¢ per person. It was this resourcefulness in utilizing every asset to its full potential that helped the company grow to the large corporation it became. (Courtesy of the Steve Port Collection.)

In this 1960s publicity shot, Clarence Garrett is shown standing in front of a double-trailer truck with the familiar block "G" logo in the background. Although Garrett and his family originated in rural Virginia, Pocatello was his home for all of his adult life. Many of his extended family members ultimately moved to Idaho, and several were employed with the company. (Courtesy of the Steve Port Collection.)

Climbing the steep, snowy terrain through the Bannock Mountain Range of Idaho, this International DCO-405 truck forges through the bitter cold to deliver its precious cargo. Garrett Freightlines established itself early as the leader in dependable, timely delivery, despite the rough terrain and frigid winter weather the company's drivers often faced. Clarence Garrett set the tone himself in 1919, when he drove 44 hours over three days (and got stuck in the mud over Malad Summit near the Idaho-Utah border) to transport a shipment of furniture from Pocatello to Salt Lake City. (Courtesy of the Steve Port Collection.)

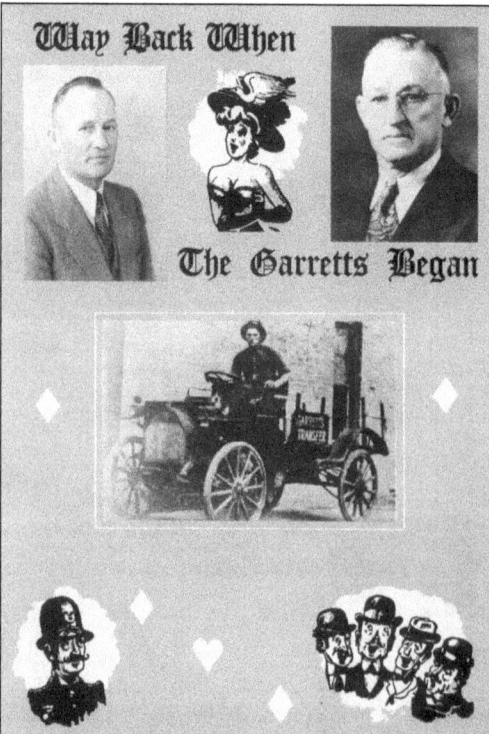

The 1913 Reo has become a symbol of the beginnings of Pocatello. Here it is pictured in front of the new, updated terminal built by Garrett Freightlines in 1951 on the street that is now known as Garrett Way. The "G" logo atop the building would continue to serve as a landmark for residents and visitors to the great Gate City of Pocatello. (Courtesy of the Lawrence Allsberry Estate Collection.)

"Way Back when the Garretts Began," written by Abrian Curtis, paints a scenic picture through joyful song of the long road driven by the loyal, dependable drivers of Garrett Freightlines. The lyrics tell a tale of two brothers who started a business that grew to become one of the largest and most widespread freight companies in America. (Courtesy of the Lawrence Allsberry Estate Collection.)

16

Clarence Garrett recognized a business opportunity when he saw the new mechanized trucks used to transport passenger luggage from the train stations in the major cities on the East Coast. In the early 1910s, Pocatello's in-city transport services were almost exclusively animal-powered, and mechanized vehicles were so unreliable that it was unclear whether they would ever be able to compete with horses. To cope with the impact of mechanical issues, Clarence Garrett established a first-class shop at the original Pocatello terminal building (above) and treated his mechanics well, including them in this early company photograph. After the company moved to the new location on Garrett Way (below), Clarence Garrett built a custom maintenance garage with luxuries such as heated floors to promote the comfort of his mechanics. (Both, courtesy of the Steve Port Collection.)

Two classics are pictured side-by-side in this staged photograph near one of the Garrett Freightlines terminals on the West Coast. Clarence Garrett always had a special place in his heart for the original 1913 Reo, despite its unreliability. This photograph, with the old Reo in front of a vintage sailing ship, highlighted the growing influence of the company as it purchased smaller freight carriers and expanded westward. (Courtesy of the Steve Port Collection.)

On display in front of the upgraded 1951 Garrett Freightlines headquarters in Pocatello are four different models of Garrett Freightlines trucks. In addition, the background shows the loading dock during the hustle and bustle of daily life at Garrett Freightlines. The photograph represents the visible evolution the company made from the early 1900s into the 1970s. (Courtesy of the Steve Port Collection.)

These scenic rock cliffs are well known in the area. This photograph was taken on the south end of Pocatello, near the lava rock formations popular with rock climbers and recreation enthusiasts in Ross Park. Pictured in front of this rock formation are a Kenworth Garrett Transfer & Storage truck and trailer. (Courtesy of the Steve Port Collection.)

Over the decades, the trucking company expanded from delivering luggage from the railroad to delivering goods all over the western United States. This delivery truck was one of many that Garrett Freightlines used for delivery. These trucks were used to transport larger loads to major metropolitan centers along the West Coast (such as Los Angeles and Emeryville, California; Portland, Oregon; and Seattle, Washington), throughout the Intermountain West (Las Vegas, Nevada; Salt Lake City, Utah; and Denver, Colorado), and eventually as far east as St. Paul, Minnesota. (Courtesy of the Lawrence Allsberry Estate Collection.)

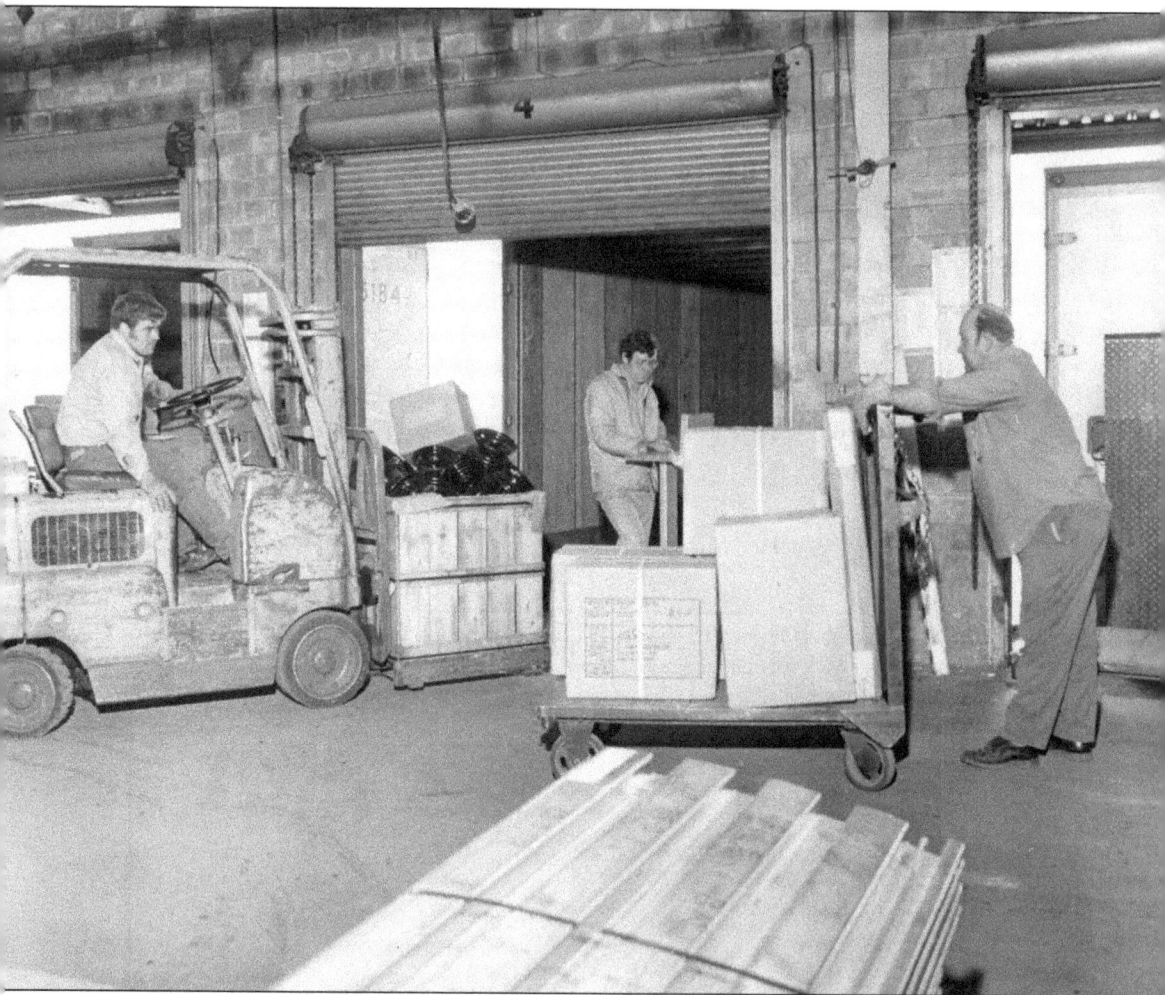

The new Garrett Freightlines Terminal complex was constructed on what is now Garrett Way in the northwest quadrant of Pocatello in 1951. The company sectioned off part of its new building for a maintenance garage. Company mechanics would change oil, rotate tires, and even rebuild trucks, piece by piece, in this building. This state-of-the-art building included heated floors in the garage to insure employee safety and comfort. Garrett Freightlines employees worked hard to provide superior service to their customers and to assure that loads of freight reached customers safely and in a timely manner. The dock workers and freight loaders pictured here were critical to the company's success, but their efforts occurred largely behind the scenes. (Courtesy of the Steve Port Collection.)

From the company's earliest days, Clarence Garrett sought to surround himself with creative and reliable mechanics who could work in the shop to rebuild and customize vehicles to meet the demands of the mountainous Intermountain West. This 1938 photograph shows the entire team of mechanics in the shop at the company's original location on First Street in Pocatello. This group of men solved the seemingly impossible task of designing a chassis both light and strong enough to support a diesel engine that could power a truck across the Great Basin to California. (Courtesy of the Lawrence Allsberry Estate Collection.)

These two Garrett trucks are decorated for a Fourth of July parade in the early 1930s. Garrett Freightlines experienced substantial growth during World Wars I and II by transporting food, supplies, and equipment to and from the West Coast to meet America's wartime logistical needs. (Courtesy of the Lawrence Allsberry Estate Collection.)

Despite growing up near the East Coast, Clarence Garrett grew to love the rugged beauty and romantic individualism of the western United States. This cover of an issue of the company newsletter, *Garrett Topics*, is an example of commissioned artwork depicting the raw, untamed natural beauty of the landscape in which Garrett Freightlines operated. (Courtesy of the Lawrence Allsberry Estate Collection.)

The most important underlying theme within Garrett Freightlines was the family of employees. Without the efforts of these employees, Garrett would not have been able to leave behind the legacy known today. Garrett owners are remembered for making employee satisfaction a top priority by constantly acknowledging their efforts and always providing a positive and motivating work environment. For that reason, many employees worked for Garrett for their entire careers. The feeling of belonging and camaraderie that Garrett employees shared is still felt. (Courtesy of the Lawrence Allsberry Estate Collection.)

Two

ORGANIZATIONAL CULTURE AND GARRETT'S PEOPLE

As many of the chapters in this book suggest, the identity of Garrett Freightlines was strongly associated with its terminals and trucks and equipment. However, it was the people who made the company, and Garrett's culture was perhaps its biggest asset. The culture did something more than give employees an enjoyable place to work; it created an environment of innovation and a belief that the company would care for its employees through hard times. Because of this, Garrett Freightlines became known as the place to start a career, offering good compensation and benefits and recognition for a fair day's work.

One of the ways that Garrett Freightlines built and reinforced its culture was through *Garrett Topics*, an internal company newsletter that came out monthly (and later quarterly). *Garrett Topics* was valuable in drawing attention to the values that Clarence Garrett sought to reinforce: recognition of safe, long-tenured, and courteous drivers; letters from customers who received outstanding service from Garrett drivers and staff; personal profiles of Garrett employees, their families, and their activities outside of work; and articles and tidbits celebrating life in the western United States. Several of the photographs in this and subsequent chapters are drawn from that publication.

The family culture that Garrett Freightlines instilled continued long after the company's demise. Groups of employees continued to hold annual reunions, reminiscing about the "good old days" and enjoying the company of former coworkers and their families. The intense feeling of nostalgia cannot be overstated. In researching this book, the authors were struck by the feelings so many former employees expressed and how sad they were when the company was sold.

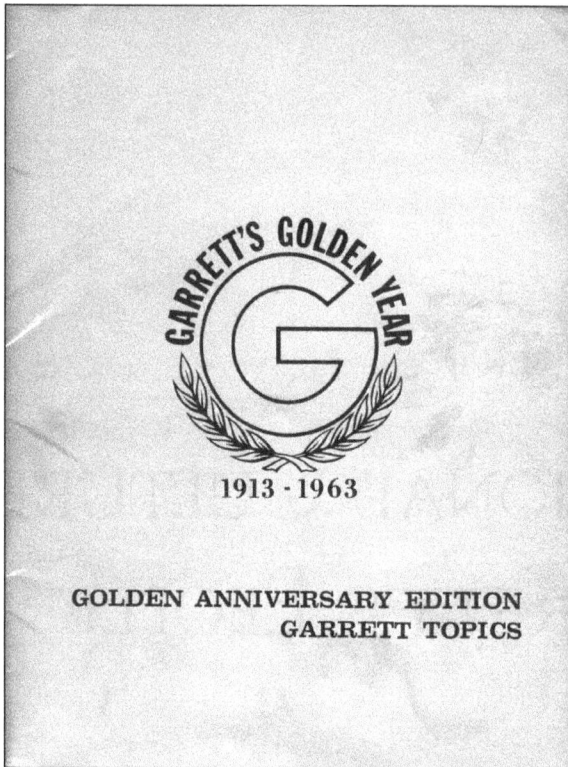

GARRETT'S GOLDEN YEAR

G

1913 - 1963

GOLDEN ANNIVERSARY EDITION
GARRETT TOPICS

This is the golden anniversary edition of *Garrett Topics*. As an internal monthly newsletter, *Garrett Topics* was one of the major ways that Garrett Freightlines transformed its business from a place to merely receive a paycheck to a truly desirable culture that enhanced the quality of employee life. Reading an issue of the newsletter offers a glimpse into the lives of those involved with the company. It showcased individual employees, their families, their children, personal and company successes, the many letters giving thanks to employees for their help in times of need, and much more. (Courtesy of the Richard J. Heinz Collection, Special Collections, Eli M. Oboler Library, Idaho State University.)

One of the many ways Garrett Freightlines tried to inspire its workers was through various mottos and catchphrases that were well publicized throughout the company. Phrases such as "make it happen" and "we do care" were used repeatedly in published materials and became part of the fabric of the company's culture. (Courtesy of the Richard J. Heinz Collection, Special Collections, Eli M. Oboler Library, Idaho State University.)

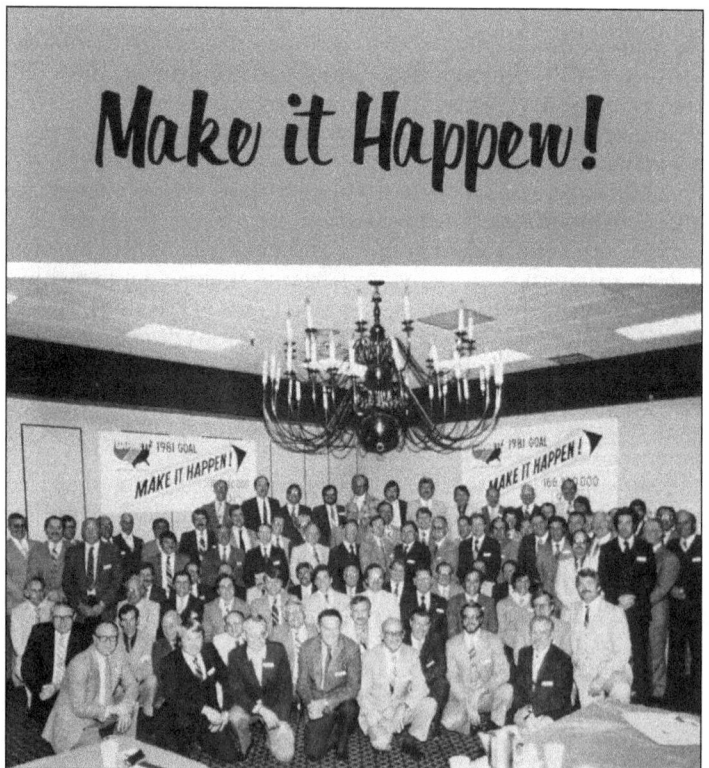

Make it Happen!

A guiding principle of Garrett Freightlines was its commitment to transparency for both employees and investors. These images from the 1957 Annual Report portray the company's commitment to its principles by fully disclosing its fiscal stability, breakdown of costs, and future monetary goals. Financial transparency was one of the tactics used by the company to foster employee trust and commitment. (Both, courtesy of the Richard J. Heinz Collection, Special Collections, Eli M. Oboler Library, Idaho State University.)

Officers and Directors

Clarence A. Garrett
President
and Founder

Wain Garrett
Vice President
Maintenance

William J. Wilson
Executive
Vice President

Ray A. Hendricks
Vice President
Sales

Norman V. Stedtfeld
Vice President-
Secretary

Carl J. Sahlberg
Director

Otto H. Tschanz, Jr.
Treasurer-
Comptroller

Maurice H. Greene
General Counsel
and Director

Ralph M. Wallace
Director and Manager
Northwest Division

Chester J. Sams
Vice President
Traffic

Lawrence M. Allsberry
Vice President
Operations

DEPARTMENT HEADS

Richard W. Anderson
Manager,
Tire Department

Bernard F. (Gus) Bengal
Assistant to VP
Operations

Ted E. Bistline
Advertising
Manager

Robert E. Bull
Operations
Manager

Clair D. Buttars
Special Agent

Louise E. Cooper
Office Manager

Howard R. Curtis
Purchasing Agent

Vincent G. Davis
Service Shop
Foreman

E. Melford Eggan
Traffic Manager
Northwest

Rex W. Geary
Operations
Manager

C. Arden Green
Director of Sales

Jack A. Green
Manager Traffic
Department

4

This page shows the leaders of Garrett Freightlines. The company was a product of its times, with a defined hierarchy. Many of the officers shown here were once line drivers and/or terminal managers at various locations throughout the western United States. William "Bill" Wilson (top row, third from left) would ultimately succeed Clarence Garrett as company president following Garrett's sudden passing. (Courtesy of the Richard J. Heinz Collection, Special Collections, Eli M. Oboler Library, Idaho State University.)

This is the Junior Board of the Garrett Freightlines Company. Clarence Garrett strongly believed in promoting from within and started training the Garrett Freightlines Company's future leaders on this board. He hoped they could learn how to run the company while maintaining the strong reputation and culture he had worked hard to achieve. (Courtesy of the Richard J. Heinz Collection, Special Collections, Eli M. Oboler Library, Idaho State University.)

Garrett Freightlines grew successfully and continually for decades. This picture is of the Garrett executives who worked to run the company in a time when there were no emails, cellphones with cameras, or texting abilities. All they had were phones that connected with an operator to get in contact with others, telegraph, or mail. (Courtesy of the Richard J. Heinz Collection, Special Collections, Eli M. Oboler Library, Idaho State University.)

Pictured is one of the numerous banquets put on throughout the years as a token of the company's appreciation for its employees, this one at the Rodeway Inn in Pocatello. Garrett believed that the company's success was derived primarily from its employees, and thus events like this were common. In fact, it was not uncommon for Clarence Garrett himself to walk around, no matter the time of day, to chat with employees and show his appreciation for their work. (Courtesy of the Richard J. Heinz Collection, Special Collections, Eli M. Oboler Library, Idaho State University.)

Certificate Of Merit

This is to certify that

is a duly accredited and honorable member of the

WE DO CARE CLUB

An exclusive organization of

GARRETT FREIGHTLINES, INC. EMPLOYEES

who exemplify the true spirit of caring. This certificate of merit and appreciation is awarded this .... day of .... 19.......
at .... with our heartiest congratulations.

_____
PRESIDENT

_____
TERMINAL MANAGER

This is one of the certificates that Garrett Freightlines would give to those who exemplified the kind of employees the company wanted. The certificate was meant to give recognition that employees could take home and show to their families. This was a definite way to help inspire others to strive for the same kind of quality. The employees were mentioned in *Garrett Topics* and commended for their service for all employees to see. (Courtesy of the Richard J. Heinz Collection, Special Collections, Eli M. Oboler Library, Idaho State University.)

One of the many ways that Garrett Freightlines created an environment that employees loved to be a part of was by recognizing the achievements of its employees, even publicizing them in *Garrett Topics* each month. The company recognized those who followed safety standards and helped others on the road and gave awards starting at an employee's five-year anniversary of employment. It was not uncommon for employees to be recognized for milestones of 35 years of service and beyond in some cases. (Courtesy of the Richard J. Heinz Collection, Special Collections, Eli M. Oboler Library, Idaho State University.)

At Garrett Freightlines, efforts were made to recognize employee contributions, regardless of whether they were male or female. Here, a woman receives an award for her dedication to "office functioning and overall commitment to the company." Constantly taking these small initiatives—recognizing employees who may otherwise be passed by—further instilled a deep love of the company among the employees. (Courtesy of the Richard J. Heinz Collection, Special Collections, Eli M. Oboler Library, Idaho State University.)

This picture from *Garrett Topics* is from a recurring feature profiling a "Garrett Girl." This section of the newsletter highlighted a female employee but sometimes mentioned things that seem sexist by today's standards, such as her height and weight or even her relationship status. Nonetheless, one of the ladies interviewed for this book expressed her pride at being recognized as a Garrett Girl. (Courtesy of the Richard J. Heinz Collection, Special Collections, Eli M. Oboler Library, Idaho State University.)

The "Garrett Teenager" section spotlighted the teenaged children of employees and recognized their achievements and goals. Articles like this were yet another means of helping Garrett Freightlines feel like it was a family where everyone was interconnected. Among the former employees interviewed for this book, most had similar things to say about liking their job and expressing the feeling that Garrett was like a family. (Courtesy of the Richard J. Heinz Collection, Special Collections, Eli M. Oboler Library, Idaho State University.)

This is a photograph of the Martinez family, one of numerous families of employees who over the years were highlighted in a monthly feature in *Garrett Topics*. Garrett Freightlines created a sense of kinship with its employees by cultivating an all-encompassing business-family culture. Until fully three decades after Garrett Freightlines was sold, former employees and their children met for yearly reunions. (Courtesy of the Richard J. Heinz Collection, Special Collections, Eli M. Oboler Library, Idaho State University.)

Larry Allsberry, the new director of operations at the Garrett Freightlines headquarters in Pocatello, oversees employees as they manually type up customer invoices. Allsberry began his career with the company as a line driver and was quickly promoted to the role of terminal manager at Pendleton, Oregon. He was then asked to move to Pocatello to oversee operations as the company expanded and began to make plans to build a new headquarters complex. (Courtesy of the Lawrence Allsberry Estate Collection.)

As a company that operated in the rapidly growing western United States, where urban growth met rural lifestyles in unexpected ways, Garrett employees sometimes saw things that would have been unknown to trucking firms on the East Coast. For instance, in this photograph, a bull from a local ranch got loose and found its way to the grounds of the Garrett terminal in Los Angeles. Local law enforcement took advantage of the fenced-in Garrett property to chase down and corral the animal and return it to its owner. (Courtesy of the Lawrence Allsberry Estate Collection.)

In keeping with the theme of Garrett Freightlines as an extended family, *Garrett Topics* occasionally featured the unusual adventures of Garrett employees' family members. In this photograph, the two sons of Garrett employee Wayne Green, Frank (left) and Dan (right), show off the two steelhead salmon they hooked on the Upper Salmon River in Idaho. Frank's catch was slightly larger than Dan's, measuring 31 inches and weighing 9.5 pounds. (Courtesy of the Lawrence Allsberry Estate Collection.)

Upon the completion of the exterior of the Minidome (now Holt Arena) in 1970, Idaho State University (ISU) had difficulty installing its scoreboards above the seats inside the building. The school called on Garrett Freightlines to find an innovative solution, which the company did. (Courtesy of the Richard J. Heinz Collection, Special Collections, Eli M. Oboler Library, Idaho State University.)

Prior to the completion of Turner Hall, one of the residence halls on ISU's campus, Garrett Freightlines assisted in moving the first set of furniture into the building. In order to complete this task, each trailer was modified to be hoisted by a crane to deliver furniture directly to each floor. Garrett Freightlines prided itself on its ability to innovate custom solutions for its customers as well as helping the local community. (Courtesy of the Richard J. Heinz Collection, Special Collections, Eli M. Oboler Library, Idaho State University.)

In 1957, Garrett Freightlines chose to donate two Buda diesel engines to the Trade and Industrial School of Idaho State College in Pocatello. The donation was meant to inspire learning of the machinery and to find ways to improve it. Garrett Freightlines had played a significant role in the development of diesel engines and wanted to strengthen connections with the university, inspire the next generation of great minds, and hopefully leave another impact on the Pocatello community. (Courtesy of the Richard J. Heinz Collection, Special Collections, Eli M. Oboler Library, Idaho State University.)

This article in *Garrett Topics* encouraged employees to get their flu shot in order to stay healthy throughout the winter months. Garrett was somewhat unique for its time in providing temporary on-site clinics to make it more convenient for employees to get their flu shots. (Courtesy of the Richard J. Heinz Collection, Special Collections, Eli M. Oboler Library, Idaho State University.)

Flu Shots, Anyone?

For the past two years the Booster Club of the Billings terminal has sponsored flue shots for the employees and their families. On Friday, October 17, Nola Goulding (wife of sleeper driver Sherman Goulding) gave her time and skill to give 72 shots. As we understand it, this was only the first of several clinics to cover all employees' families, this eliminating a major cause for absenteeism in schools and from work.

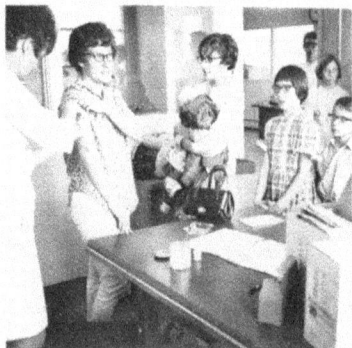

Mrs. Don Knote restrains son Richard while Mrs. George Barry and daughter wait in line for flu shots administered by Nurse Nola Goulding.

Family of Sleeper Driver Eugene Johnstone get flu shots from Nola Goulding, wife of another Sleeper Driver, Sherm Goulding.

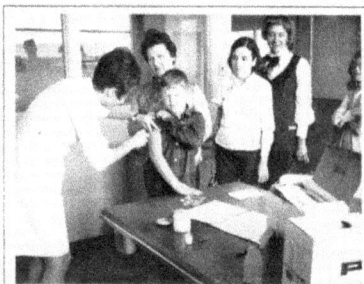

Garrett Freightlines was involved in much more than just the lives of those it employed. Garrett hoped to expand its boundaries to many forms of media that would help to entertain and build the communities in which it functioned. The *High Adventure* episode "Cannonball" was just one of the things it helped to fund. (Courtesy of the Richard J. Heinz Collection, Special Collections, Eli M. Oboler Library, Idaho State University.)

Garrett Sponsors TV Program

Eyes firmly peeled for hazards ahead, Paul Birch and William Campbell portray Mike "Cannonball" Malone and his partner Jerry Austin in "CANNONBALL," the thrill-packed story of high adventure.

Clarence Garrett believed in civic responsibility and took the opportunity to encourage his employees and the Pocatello community to get out and vote on Election Day. This photograph shows an advertisement posted on the side of Garrett trailers reminding citizens to vote. (Courtesy of the Richard J. Heinz Collection, Special Collections, Eli M. Oboler Library, Idaho State University.)

IS THIS YOU?

The word **"IDIOT"** comes from a Greek word meaning

"THE MAN WHO DID NOT VOTE"

The man who does not vote may be - unintentionally - serving the MACHINE BOSSES, PRESSURE GROUPS, CROOKS AND BAD GOVERMENTS in general.

SO--

For Government OF THE PEOPLE
BY THE PEOPLE
FOR THE PEOPLE

REGISTER AND VOTE!

This item, placed strategically on the back cover of an edition of *Garrett Topics*, was one of the many examples of things Garrett Freightlines put in its publications to encourage employees to be politically active. Regardless of how people voted, this item provides more evidence that Clarence Garrett felt voting was a civic duty, not just a choice. (Courtesy of the Richard J. Heinz Collection, Special Collections, Eli M. Oboler Library, Idaho State University.)

Two Garrett Freightlines executives are seen here placing signs on a Garrett truck that has been loaned out to help collect clothes for the Goodwill School Clothing Drive. The company loaned out its trucks to help with community fundraisers and to build goodwill. It was not uncommon to see Garrett employees themselves playing crucial roles in these fundraisers. (Courtesy of the Richard J. Heinz Collection, Special Collections, Eli M. Oboler Library, Idaho State University.)

The employees of Garrett Freightlines worked and lived in a culture where caring for the community was not only highly valued but was almost an unstated expectation. Pictured are three Garrett Freightlines employees who committed themselves to serve the local community as volunteer firefighters. This commitment from employees contributed to making Garrett Freightlines a beloved company in the cities it served. (Courtesy of the Richard J. Heinz Collection, Special Collections, Eli M. Oboler Library, Idaho State University.)

The sleek, stylish designs of Garrett Freightlines trucks and equipment were a source of pride for Garrett employees and an inspiration for truck enthusiasts around the United States. This model truck was built by Ronald Posselt of Appleton, Wisconsin, a state that was east of Garrett's service area. A number of individuals scattered across the country continue to collect Garrett models, photographs, and memorabilia, keeping the memory of Garrett Freightlines alive. (Courtesy of the Lawrence Allsberry Estate Collection.)

Three

TRUCKS AND EQUIPMENT

The iconic green-and-yellow "G" served as the symbol of Garrett Freightlines, but it was the trucks that many former employees and industry enthusiasts have the fondest memories of. The trucks, and those who drove them, became a regular sight on the many highways and byways of the western half of the United States, driving their way into countless children's memories and road-trip stories. To those who were passing them on the highway, a Garrett truck served as a reminder of progress, of a continual drive to reach a destination, and a reflection of the ethic of America itself.

Garrett Freightlines took pride in its equipment. The company was involved in developing some of the most impressive advances in the transportation industry during the 20th century. Garrett was a pioneer of the idea that a company can actively partner with its suppliers, including Goodyear, US Rubber, Firestone, Goodrich, Kenworth, Mack Trucks, and Cummins, to produce noteworthy innovations (including lightweight diesel engines, refrigerated trailers, specialized equipment capable of hauling hazardous materials safely, and triple trailers) and continuously improve the quality of engines, tires, axles, and other component parts. These partnerships varied in depth and duration, with the developments frequently requiring project specialists and engineers from multiple organizations.

Creating this competitive advantage through continuous innovation was no accident; it was part of Garrett Freightlines' business strategy from the beginning. Some questioned whether motorized vehicles would ever be reliable enough to replace horses in the 1910s, so Clarence Garrett's purchase of a half-ton, one-cylinder 1913 Reo truck was a risk. However, the company could have only guessed that its key business strategy would become associated with the population expansion of the United States. This chapter pays homage to the memories of the thousands who passed Garrett Freightlines trucks on the highway, pumping their fists in anticipation of a tugged air horn.

Driving a Garrett Freightlines truck was a good and stable job, even in uncertain times. Pictured here are some of the drivers who operated the trucks on various routes across the western United States. Proudly standing next to their rigs, some even wearing ties, these drivers knew the importance of their jobs. When people were hired at Garrett Freightlines, it was common for them to stay with the company for the remainder of their careers. (Courtesy of the Lawrence Allsberry Estate Collection.)

Sometimes the cost of innovation is looking a little unusual. This was the case with this short-wheelbase, cab-beside-engine tractor, built to host a single driver in order to minimize wasted space. While it was not an everyday occurrence to see these type of trucks, they were not terribly uncommon, since they were especially useful to transport oddly shaped freight. Additionally, removing the passenger side of the cab eliminated more than 500 pounds of mostly unused space, increasing the overall fuel economy of the tractor. (Courtesy of the Lawrence Allsberry Estate Collection.)

This Kenworth three-axle tractor was equipped with a 252-horsepower diesel engine, air brake system, and 10-speed transmission. This one is hauling a trailer manufactured by Brown Division of Clark Equipment Company. The trailer's overall length was 60 feet, and it was 13.5 feet tall. Diesel engines for Garrett's large trucks were developed in collaboration with Cummins Inc. for extended exposure in high-temperature routes. (Courtesy of the Lawrence Allsberry Estate Collection.)

A Garrett truck with a fixed van body was a common sight around town, as it was commonly used for local deliveries. Although Garrett owned many trucking routes that crossed state lines, it always maintained a local presence. Not missing an opportunity to advertise the company's services, the truck announced a faster service option for potential future customers both in Pocatello and other communities. (Courtesy of the Lawrence Allsberry Estate Collection.)

Pictured here is an International two-axle tractor. Their engines produced 172 horsepower and were commonly combined with a four-speed transmission. They are attached to Pike trailers that were 27 feet, 3 inches long and held a payload capacity of 44,000 pounds. Trucks like these were primarily used to make local deliveries and were produced by the Ford Motor Company. (Courtesy of the Lawrence Allsberry Estate Collection.)

This Garrett Freightlines tractor was made by Kenworth and was labeled with the identification number 21-182. Units like this were often used for flatbed operations and hauled specialized equipment, machinery, and other loads requiring large space or weight capacities. In the later years of Garrett Freightlines, the competition grew fierce, and the company searched for new market opportunities. The search led to equipment like this tractor and triple-trailer trucks to expand hauling capacities for new markets. (Courtesy of the Steve Port Collection.)

This photograph shows Garrett Freightlines Kenworth truck no. 65. Advertisements of the company's capabilities and services were painted on either side of the truck along with location destinations. This particular truck is equipped with a sleeper cab, allowing transportation of cargo over long distances while providing the drivers with some amenities. (Courtesy of the Steve Port Collection.)

Triple-trailer trucks required a lot of work in layout and design for safety and drivability. The triples actually had remarkable safety ratings and cut down on fuel costs up to 27 percent. Today, a triple-trailer is a fairly common sight on the freeway. Garrett was the first to debut this technology on the roads and proudly declared the project a success during its time. (Courtesy of the Lawrence Allsberry Estate Collection.)

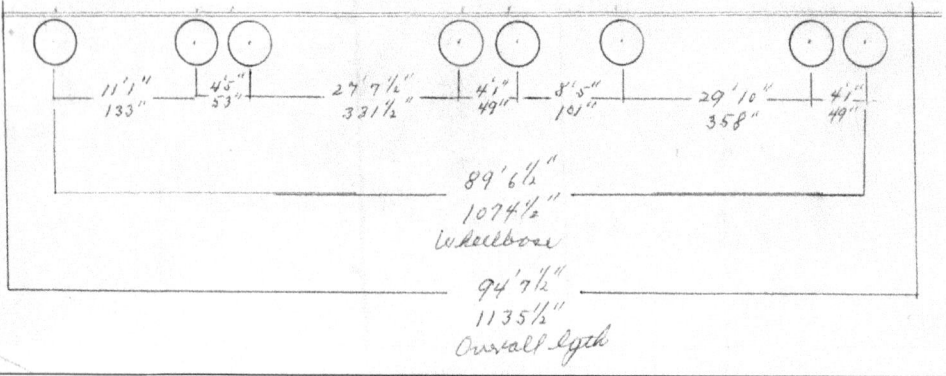

GARRETT FREIGHTLINES, INC.
INTER-OFFICE CORRESPONDENCE

FORM 4-R1

3 axle tractor
PIE 40 footer
Garrett 40 footer

TO *used in Nevada tests week of Jan 8-12 1968* DATE
CC

FROM AT CC

REFERENCE *23-907* *PIE*

11'1" *4'5"* *27'7½"* *4'5"* *8'5"* *29'10"* *4'1"*
133" *53"* *331½"* *49"* *101"* *358"* *49"*

89'6½"
1074½"
wheelbase

94'7½"
1135½"
Overall length

After a long period of testing and lobbying for permission from state trucking commissions in several western states, the three-trailer truck configuration was approved to operate on state highways, Nevada being the first state to grant permission. Pictured here are two of the records documenting the extensive process of checking and rechecking all aspects of the triple trailer, including weight distribution, length of spacing, and length of trailer. The initial investment of time and money paid off, as the introduction of the triple trailer continued to establish Garrett's reputation as a leader in the industry. (Both, courtesy of the Steve Port Collection.)

GARRETT FREIGHTLINES, INC.
INTER-OFFICE CORRESPONDENCE

4-R1

DATE 4-9-68

TO Audie Webb Las Vegas
    Cid Harr AT Twin Falls CC Bob Barta, Pocatello
                              CC
FROM L. M. Allsberry AT Pocatello CC

REFERENCE Triple experiment

A 60 day extension has been granted in the experimental operation of triples
on US 93 between Las Vegas and Twin Falls. This extension granted by the
State of Nevada will permit us to operate to June 7, 1968

44

This advertisement shows a variety of trucks and trailers Garrett Freightlines operated, as well as some of the features of each truck. Garrett Freightlines maintained high customer and employee satisfaction ratings as a company and communicated new equipment development to customers to ensure them that it would meet their needs. This advertisement highlights how Garrett Freightlines replaced trucks without hesitation if they failed to meet the company's safety standards. (Courtesy of the Lawrence Allsberry Estate Collection.)

Garrett Freightlines took pride in its ability to transport various cargoes. Pictured here with visible "FLAMMABLE" signage is a tractor hauling three fuel trailers. Governments and large corporations often approached Garrett to transport hazardous materials and other cargo that required specialized safety precautions because of the company's established history of safe driving and delivery. (Courtesy of the Lawrence Allsberry Estate Collection.)

To accommodate an assortment of cargo loads of various shapes, sizes, and weights, Garrett Freightlines designed and commissioned numerous trailer designs that were capable of several different applications. Here, a trailer attached to a hydraulic lift and equipped with a removable top cover was used in the process of loading and unloading various cargoes, especially within the agriculture industry. (Courtesy of the Lawrence Allsberry Estate Collection.)

The power units of Garrett Freightlines were not the only equipment to get attention from the company. Garrett Freightlines made continuous design improvements to the trailers the power units were hauling. This trailer, photographed on May 17, 1957, had a removable top and dual access doors. These types of trailers were versatile and could be transported almost anywhere, with ample storage space for multiple cargoes. (Courtesy of the Lawrence Allsberry Estate Collection.)

A Truck Everyone Likes(?)

What the OWNER wants...

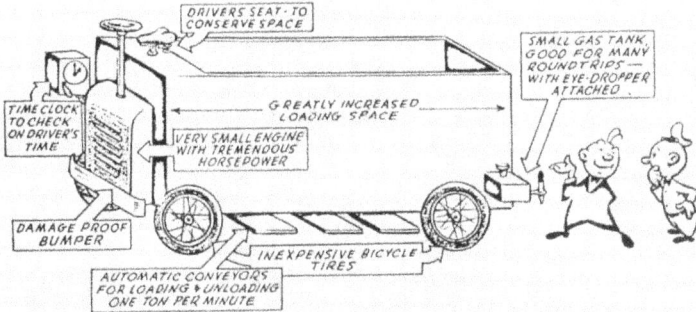

DRIVERS SEAT - TO CONSERVE SPACE

SMALL GAS TANK, GOOD FOR MANY ROUND TRIPS — WITH EYE-DROPPER ATTACHED

TIME CLOCK TO CHECK ON DRIVER'S TIME

GREATLY INCREASED LOADING SPACE

VERY SMALL ENGINE WITH TREMENDOUS HORSEPOWER

DAMAGE PROOF BUMPER

INEXPENSIVE BICYCLE TIRES

AUTOMATIC CONVEYORS FOR LOADING & UNLOADING ONE TON PER MINUTE

What the MECHANIC wants...

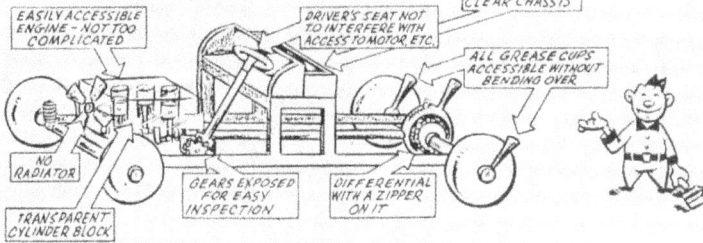

TRUCK BODY - TO CLEAR CHASSIS

EASILY ACCESSIBLE ENGINE - NOT TOO COMPLICATED

DRIVER'S SEAT NOT TO INTERFERE WITH ACCESS TO MOTOR, ETC.

ALL GREASE CUPS ACCESSIBLE WITHOUT BENDING OVER

NO RADIATOR

TRANSPARENT CYLINDER BLOCK

GEARS EXPOSED FOR EASY INSPECTION

DIFFERENTIAL WITH A ZIPPER ON IT

What the DRIVER wants...

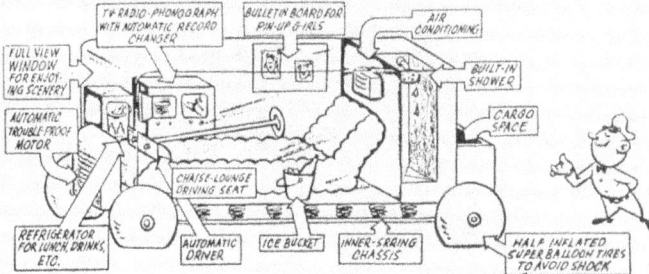

TV RADIO PHONOGRAPH WITH AUTOMATIC RECORD CHANGER

BULLETIN BOARD FOR PIN-UP GIRLS

AIR CONDITIONING

FULL VIEW WINDOW FOR ENJOYING SCENERY

BUILT-IN SHOWER

AUTOMATIC TROUBLE-PROOF MOTOR

CARGO SPACE

CHAISE-LOUNGE DRIVING SEAT

REFRIGERATOR FOR LUNCH, DRINKS, ETC.

AUTOMATIC DRIVER

ICE BUCKET

INNER-SPRING CHASSIS

HALF INFLATED SUPER BALLOON TIRES TO AVOID SHOCK

This cartoon gives a pictorial description of the challenges of ordering trucks that adequately served the needs of various stakeholders. Each truck was designed to meet the needs of customers, the engineers who were in charge of managing the mechanical operations of the trucks, and the drivers who drove them. (Courtesy of the Lawrence Allsberry Estate Collection.)

47

Garrett Freightlines was contracted by a number of companies to transport highly specialized cargoes. Pictured above in June 1963 is a General Electric Test Reactor (GETR) Fuel Shipping Cask that was used to transport radioactive material from Visalia, California, to Scoville, Idaho. The safe transportation of cargo like this required highly qualified drivers and careful customization to make sure the equipment was up to the task. Larry Allsberry, Garrett Freightlines' vice president of operations, calculated that the available axles in the special flatbed Garrett truck could accommodate shipping casks of no more than 24,000 pounds. The weight certificate attached to this GETR shows that each cask weighed in at 23,620 pounds. (Both, courtesy of the Lawrence Allsberry Estate Collection.)

A Garrett Freightlines double-trailer refrigeration truck could be used to transport frozen goods across the United States. In the late 1930s, Garrett was among the first in the industry to use mechanically refrigerated trailers to transport perishables. This innovation allowed the company to carry fresh fruits and vegetables from the West Coast to inland destinations and pioneered opportunities for the frozen food industry. (Courtesy of the Jack Wenske Collection, Special Collections, Eli M. Oboler Library, Idaho State University)

Another Garrett breakthrough was the use of diesel fuel in the company's trucks. Extreme terrain and high temperatures along routes in the Mojave Desert made it impossible for a gasoline-powered truck to withstand the conditions. When manufacturers were reluctant to help Garrett Freightlines customize these diesel-powered trucks, the company bought diesel engines itself and customized the engines in its shop. Eventually, Garrett partnered with Cummins in Indiana and Kenworth Equipment near Seattle to produce diesel trucks on a larger scale. (Courtesy of the Lawrence Allsberry Estate Collection.)

Terminals that had service bays for the equipment also housed inspection teams that would sign off the equipment after quality tests. These bays also served as meeting points for Garrett Freightlines suppliers, who participated in collaborative projects with the company. Meticulous records of tire damage, mileage traveled, the location of the vehicle, and route paths were kept and shared with several companies. Tire companies such as Goodyear, Goodrich, American Rubber, and Firestone utilized this information for development of their own products. (Courtesy of the Steve Port Collection.)

Pictured is a White Freightliner cab-over-engine (COE) unit. It is being fitted with a rebuilt diesel Cummins engine by Garrett machinists. In the background, a Kenworth Conventional and two Emeryville Internationals are also being worked on. Several Garrett Freightlines terminals were capable of maintaining the operational functions of heavy equipment, as the company liked to keep the repair and maintenance of equipment in-house. A few of the terminals had the capability to do complete overhauls of tractors like the ones pictured here. (Courtesy of the Steve Port Collection.)

A Garrett Freightlines electrician works on a Buda engine that is installed in a COE tractor. Due to the variety of engines, tractors, and transmissions utilized by Garrett Freightlines, each shop mechanic went through an extensive training program within the company. The continuous introduction of new equipment challenged mechanics to regularly update their equipment as well as the knowledge and methods that they used. (Courtesy of the Steve Port Collection.)

Four

TERMINALS

As Garrett Freightlines expanded further into the western United States, the company needed additional terminals to support its growing network of trade routes. These terminals were used to service Garrett trucks and as checkpoints for Garrett drivers and distribution centers. They also served as regional economic supporters, local landmarks, and direction providers for more than a few lost citizen drivers.

Business strategy and government regulations played a large role in the establishment of Garrett Freightlines terminals all over the western half of the country. In the era of the regulated trucking industry, freight carriers had to obtain authority from the federal government to operate between destinations on interstate highways. In exchange for being able to operate between more lucrative metropolitan centers, freight carriers were required to also serve smaller communities on less profitable routes. As a consequence, Garrett Freightlines operated massive terminals in cities like Los Angeles and tiny terminals in towns like Mackay, Idaho.

Because terminals were the operation bases of Garrett Freightlines and allowed the company to function effectively, each terminal was designed to accommodate specific needs based on its location. Some terminals could fully overhaul an entire tractor in less than 72 hours, while others were strategically placed to provide fuel. However, all were equally important in ensuring that Garrett Freightlines cargo arrived at its destination in a safe and timely manner.

The original terminal on the 800 block of South First Street served Garrett Freightlines loyally through the company's first four decades. The terminal began as a single building, but by 1944, as Garrett grew rapidly, the company expanded to the surrounding buildings until it occupied the full block. (Courtesy of the Steve Port Collection.)

By 1919, Garrett Freightlines serviced a 50-mile radius around Pocatello. During World War I, Garrett felt pressure to expand routes from intracity to intercity. The company had previously thought of itself as primarily a baggage, furniture, and storage transfer services company. By 1921, Garrett was servicing Idaho Falls, Twin Falls, Pocatello, and Salt Lake City, making it a legitimate, competitive freight company. (Courtesy of the Historic Photographs Collection, Special Collections, Eli M. Oboler Library, Idaho State University.)

Garrett Freightlines expanded its service area to include Burley, Idaho, in 1927. In 1928, Garrett established its first out-of-state terminal in Salt Lake City. Two years later, the company continued its expansion to Butte, Montana, and maintained steady growth throughout the western United States in the succeeding decades. By the early 1960s, Garrett trucks lined the highways with the addition of routes to Los Angeles, San Francisco–Oakland, Denver, and New Mexico. During expansion, terminals in Spokane, Seattle, and Great Falls were purchased, adding to the Garrett family. (Courtesy of the Steve Port Collection.)

This photograph shows the daily receipt and delivery of shipments at the loading docks of the original Garrett Freightlines terminal on South First Street in Pocatello. The truck shows the company's original name, Garrett Transfer & Storage Company. At the time of this photograph from around the late 1930s, the original terminal building sat in a bustling commercial district across the street from the first Pocatello department and mercantile stores. (Courtesy of the Steve Port Collection.)

This image shows what the East Side warehouse district of Pocatello looked like in 1939. The original Garrett Freightlines terminal was built in close proximity to the railroad. The location of the terminal allowed for quick delivery and conservation of resources. The company used this terminal as its main operational headquarters until the business expanded and outgrew the original terminal in the early 1950s. (Courtesy of the Steve Port Collection.)

Garrett Freightlines headquarters were moved to 2055 Garrett Way and built on 22 acres. The estimated cost of the building in 1951 was $800,000 (the equivalent of approximately $7.5 million in 2016). The office building includes 15 offices and a communication room that allowed for telecommunications with all major terminals. These offices are still in use and are rented out by multiple companies. The photograph above is an aerial shot of the new terminal complex in the mid-1950s. The photograph below shows the property as it looks today. Due to the great quality in the building materials, only minor changes and fixes have had to be made to the buildings. (Above, courtesy of the Lawrence Allsberry Estate Collection; below, courtesy of Tyler Cantrell.)

Thanks to a partnership with Cummins and Kenworth to develop a lightweight diesel engine powerful enough to navigate the Mojave Desert without overheating, Garrett Freightlines was able to successfully establish a new route to Los Angeles on February 1, 1935. The race was on because, in order to be awarded regulatory authority to run the Pocatello–to–Los Angeles route, Garrett had to demonstrate its ability to complete the trip successfully before the Federal Motor Carrier Act of 1935 (the first legislation regulating which carriers had authority to serve routes between major US cities) went into effect in July of that year. In addition to the newly acquired Los Angeles route, Garrett Freightlines was able to begin runs to Portland and other cities in Oregon with the purchase of Chaney Brothers Truck Line. (Courtesy of the Lawrence Allsberry Estate Collection.)

From the passage of the Federal Motor Carrier Act of 1935 until the deregulation of the trucking industry in the early 1980s, freight lines were required to obtain authority from the Interstate Commerce Commission (ICC) to be able to deliver freight between specific cities. Garrett Freightlines discovered that the easiest way to increase its service area was by acquiring other truck lines that already had authority through the ICC. Through a series of acquisitions during the 1940s and 1950s, Garrett Freightlines was able to operate from the eastern edge of the Rocky Mountains (and ultimately St. Paul) to the ports of the West Coast of the United States. (Courtesy of the Lawrence Allsberry Estate Collection.)

Clarence Garrett believed in community involvement and made it a key part of the culture he created. This photograph of the terminal in Spokane includes advertisements on the sides of trucks encouraging citizens to vote in the upcoming presidential elections, a reflection of the emphasis the company placed on civic duty. (Courtesy of the Steve Port Collection.)

Garrett Freightlines operated large terminals in cities throughout the western United States. Unlike many freight carriers, which would locate their terminals downtown in warehouse districts where the cost of land was least expensive, Garrett sought to purchase land for its terminals closer to major roadways. This land ultimately became quite valuable over time. Today, for instance, the site of Garrett's terminal off Interstate 80 in Emeryville, California, houses an Apple store and a shopping mall while sitting only blocks from Pixar Animation's headquarters. (Courtesy of the David Faust Collection, Special Collections, Eli M. Oboler Library, Idaho State University.)

In this March 1963 photograph, the Garrett Freightlines terminal in Mount Vernon, Washington, is shown with employees busy at work preparing to fulfill a shipment. Mount Vernon was an example of a smaller Garrett terminal, with seven employees and eight pickup and delivery units (six trucks and two tractors) sitting on one acre. Severine "Si" Knudson was the terminal manager. (Courtesy of the Steve Port Collection.)

Two of the smallest terminals in the Garrett Freightlines family were at Mackay, Idaho, and Miles City, Montana. Terminals like these typically required only one or two employees to run the operation. Today these locations are served by companies such as UPS or Federal Express, but at the time, Garrett Freightlines met an important need for the western United States' smallest rural communities. The Miles City terminal is pictured above, and an unidentified Mackay terminal manager is below. (Both, courtesy of the Lawrence Allsberry Estate Collection.)

The Salt Lake City terminal was located on Redwood Road. This terminal was managed by Jack S. Christensen and had 314 regular employees. The dock space was 21,430 square feet, and the terminal was built on 22 acres. This terminal was highly profitable and was the first Garrett terminal located outside Idaho. (Courtesy of the Richard J. Heinz Collection, Special Collections, Eli M. Oboler Library, Idaho State University.)

After its expansion south to Salt Lake City, Garrett Freightlines set its sights on crossing the Idaho-Montana border. The company expanded north to Butte in 1930, where it could meet the demand for transporting raw materials from the city's copper mines. This photograph shows one of Garrett's Kenworth trucks pulling a trailer from the recently-purchased Cotant Truck Lines. (Courtesy of the Steve Port Collection.)

At the time of Garrett Freightlines' 50th anniversary, the Salmon, Idaho, terminal was managed by Murl McNabb. The terminal was not a large operation: it had two regular employees and one local pickup and delivery unit. The dock and storage space were both 2,400 square feet, and the terminal sat on half an acre of land. (Courtesy of the Richard J. Heinz Collection, Special Collections, Eli M. Oboler Library, Idaho State University.)

Until the early 1960s, the Denver terminal served as the easternmost terminal for Garrett Freightlines. It rested on a 7.7-acre lot and employed on average 89 people. After a number of acquisitions, Garrett was able to expand its services farther east to St. Paul. Due to ICC regulations, Garrett was able to provide service all the way to St. Paul but could not service any cities along the way. (Both, courtesy of the Lawrence Allsberry Estate Collection.)

The Las Vegas (above) and Boise (below) terminals seen in these photographs from the early 1960s harken back to a time when Pocatello had much greater stature among cities in the western United States. In 1950, Pocatello had a larger population than Las Vegas. As recently as 1963, when Garrett Freightlines celebrated its 50th anniversary, Pocatello was the largest city in the state of Idaho, outpacing even Boise. Whereas Pocatello's population has grown minimally, today both Boise and Las Vegas have grown into very large cities. (Both, courtesy of the Lawrence Allsberry Estate Collection.)

In 1963, Ogden, Utah, was similar to Pocatello in that both were important stops on the Union Pacific Railroad, which fueled their growth. However, Garrett's terminal in Ogden was relatively small, built on a lot that was just shy of an acre. On the south end of the state of Utah, the terminal in Moab had eight pickup and delivery units and nine employees, enough for a full-time terminal manager (Rodney Phillips, the Moab terminal manager in the late 1960s, shown here). (Both, courtesy of the Lawrence Allsberry Estate Collection.)

The terminal in Pendleton was strategically important as a stop on old US Highway 30 between the western border of Idaho and Portland. During World War II, Garrett Freightlines shipped blankets and military uniforms from the famed Pendleton Woolen Mills to the West Coast to be transported to troops on the front lines in Europe and Asia. Clarence Garrett liked to promote managers from within the company, and terminals in remote locations were valuable on-the-job training for aspiring managers. Larry Allsberry, who ultimately ascended to president of Garrett Freightlines, began his career as a terminal manager at Pendleton. (Courtesy of the Lawrence Allsberry Estate Collection.)

The population of Reno, Nevada, more than doubled from approximately 21,000 people before World War II to over 51,000 in 1960. It was more than Reno's size that made its terminal (above) important to Garrett Freightlines, however. Reno was the last stop east of Donner's Summit, the treacherous pass through the Sierra Nevada Mountains on old US Highway 40 (part of the continent-wide Lincoln Highway) to the terminal in Sacramento (below) and on to the Bay Area. In difficult winters, it was not unusual for drivers to get snowed in at Truckee, California, for a week or more at a time. (Both, courtesy of the Lawrence Allsberry Estate Collection.)

As the trucking industry matured in the 1950s and 1960s, it became harder to apply to the ICC for authority to run a route unless a freight carrier purchased an established company that already served that route. Garrett Freightlines was able to build terminals in Seattle (above) and Great Falls, Montana (below), only after purchasing companies with authority on those routes. (Both, courtesy of the Lawrence Allsberry Estate Collection.)

Lewiston is located in the panhandle of northern Idaho near the border with the state of Washington. Unlike terminals located at higher altitudes in much of the Intermountain West, the Garrett terminal in Lewiston sat at only about 700 feet above sea level, leading to a much milder climate. The article in *Garrett Topics* accompanying the photograph above described Lewiston as the "banana belt" of the western United States. The Garrett terminal at Lewiston was particularly important because Lewiston serves as an inland port (right), with ships traveling to and from the Pacific Ocean on the Columbia River. (Both, courtesy of the Lawrence Allsberry Estate Collection.)

After American Natural Resources (ANR) purchased Garrett Freightlines in 1978, the company proceeded with its plans to expand Garrett's presence in the upper midwestern United States. In 1982, ANR opened terminals throughout North and South Dakota, Minnesota, and Iowa. The new terminal building in Fargo, North Dakota, is pictured here. (Courtesy of the Lawrence Allsberry Estate Collection.)

Five

SAFETY

One of the central tenets of the culture at Garrett Freightlines was safety. Perhaps Clarence Garrett cared so much about safety because he had been seriously injured (and subsequently dismissed) while working for Union Pacific Railroad before starting his company. Or it could be that he had found that a safe company made for a profitable company. Either way, the safety precautions at Garrett Freightlines were among the best in the nation and set the standard within the transportation industry.

Safety procedures were practiced in every sector of Garrett Freightlines according to company guidelines. Detailed records of injuries, accidents, and working environments were mandatory and served as catalysts for future company safety policies. As a result, every Garrett employee was subject to countless safety awareness campaigns that ran within and outside of the company. However, safety was not prescribed in a top-down, iron-fisted manner. Instead, the Garrett approach was to recognize employees for their accomplishments in safety, often publishing their stories in issues of *Garrett Topics*, while maintaining strict accountability for breaches of safety practices. This approach empowered employees to take responsibility, ultimately making safety objectives more meaningful for them and effective for the company.

To encourage the companywide commitment to safety, Garrett Freightlines posted billboards, celebrated individual achievements, and offered incentive bonuses. Yet, along with the good, Garrett Freightlines didn't hide from the bad. Photographs of accidents and wreckage were spread right alongside the celebratory material to serve as reminders of safety lapses. The company was not averse to calling out unsafe employee behaviors in its internal newsletter. This dedication to safety served Garrett Freightlines in multiple ways. Safety tests conducted on equipment often decided which companies were awarded Garrett Freightlines' business. This led to partnerships between Garrett Freightlines and the engineering departments of several big-name companies. In turn, these companies became more invested in Garrett Freightlines and in the company's own safety measures.

From its beginnings, Garrett emphasized safety as an important aspect of its operations. Not only did Garrett Freightlines promote safety, it celebrated it, setting the company apart from other firms in the trucking industry. Safety practices were not forced on employees in a negative way but instead became part of the company's culture. Garrett Freightlines was very well known for safety throughout the industry, and awards such as these were a way to recognize employees and reinforce safe behaviors. (Courtesy of the Lawrence Allsberry Estate Collection.)

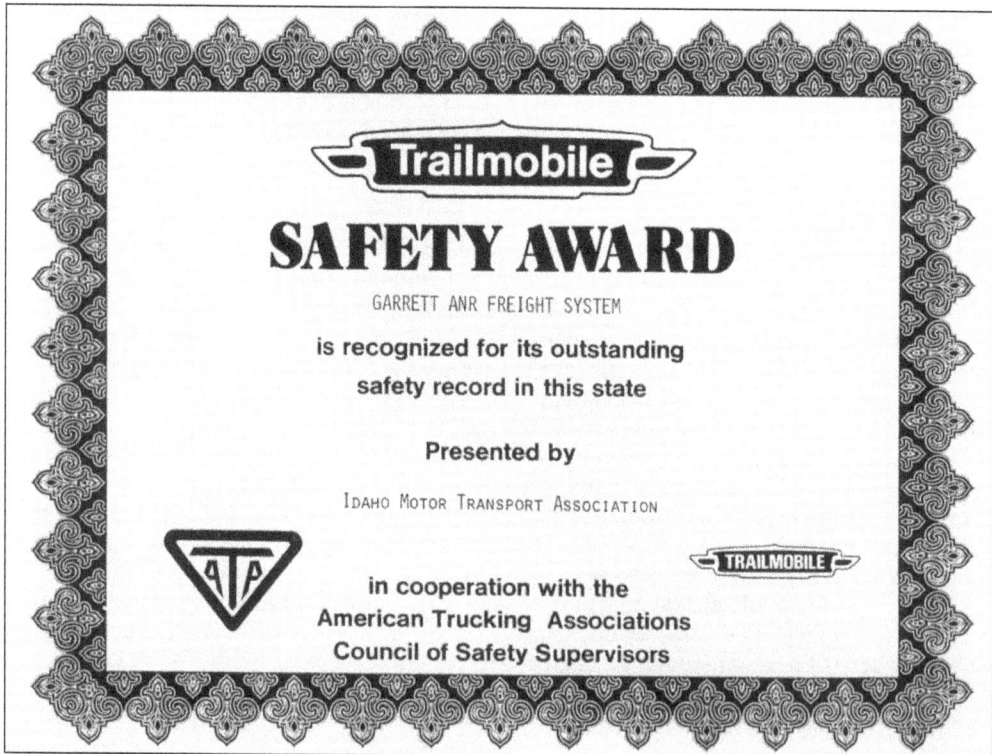

It is one thing to prioritize certain company goals and another to achieve them. Garrett was successful on both counts, earning it recognition by the Idaho State Motor Company. This gesture could be seen as further encouragement to continue with its hard work and dedication towards reducing accidents and injuries. (Courtesy of the Lawrence Allsberry Estate Collection.)

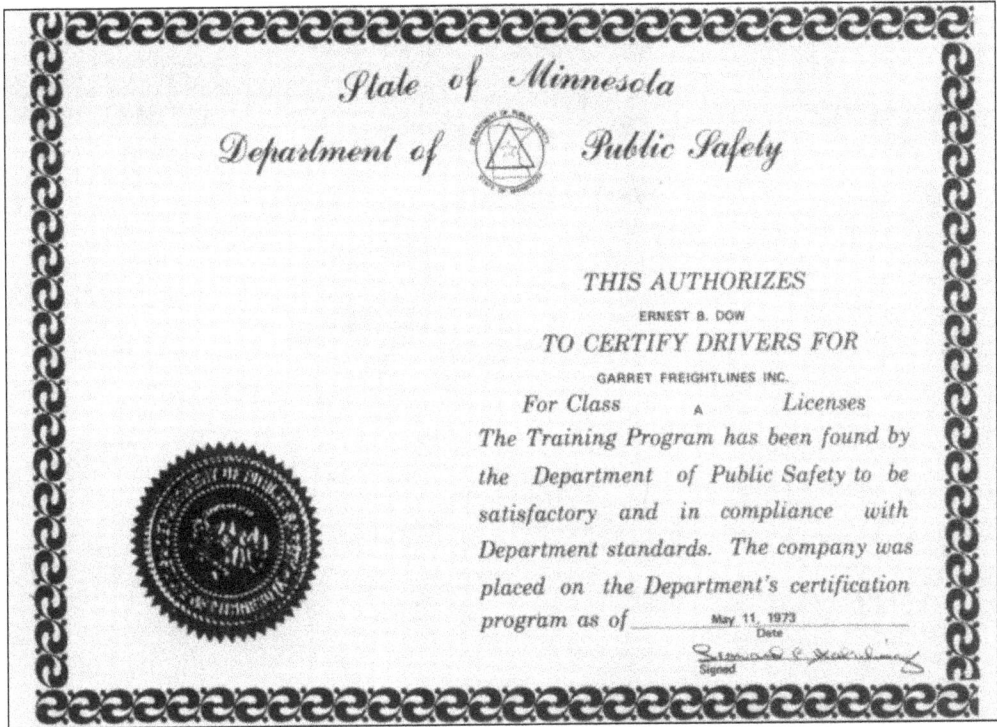

Safety amongst drivers was a top priority. Drivers like Ernie Dow received a certificate (pictured above) for completing a Class A license program. The awarding of this license ensured that each Garrett driver was well-versed in the operation and handling of the trucks he operated. Drivers would often receive certificates like these from both local and state driving departments. (Courtesy of the Lawrence Allsberry Estate Collection.)

Every driver in the company was given a driver's manual that detailed many safety regulations, including truck speed. Clarence Garrett established that drivers would not exceed 55 miles per hour, even if the road permitted higher speeds. Many trucks were equipped with a device called a tachograph that recorded a driver's speed. A former Garrett employee recounts stories of drivers that would rubber band this device to stay at 55 miles per hour even when driving above that speed. Though this story seems comical, a terminal employee would always quickly race out to incoming trucks to check the device and ensure there had been no tampering. If an employee was caught violating a safety rule, he was often suspended for a day from work. (Courtesy of the Lawrence Allsberry Estate Collection.)

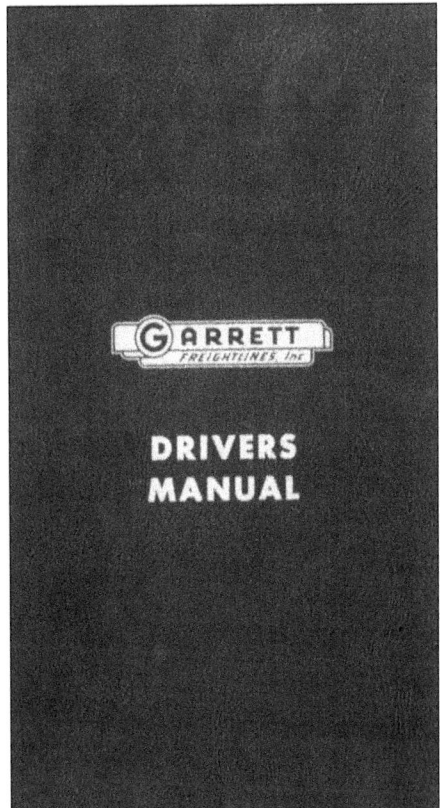

GARRETT
FREIGHTLINES, Inc.

DRIVERS
MANUAL

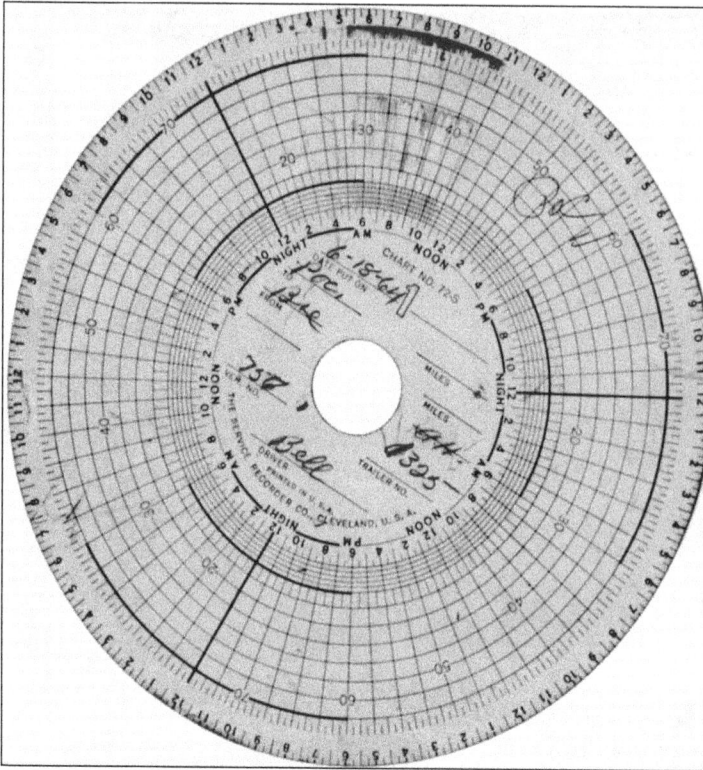

Pictured here is the tachograph that recorded the speed and distance traveled by a driver between Boise and Pocatello in June 1964. In the days before global positioning systems, tachographs were locked into a device within the truck and allowed the company to track driver speed. (Courtesy of the Lawrence Allsberry Estate Collection.)

Due to an oil shortage in 1974, a nationwide mandatory truck speed of 55 miles per hour was imposed to save fuel. However, this mandate didn't help Garrett Freightlines save oil, because it already required drivers to drive at a maximum of 55 miles per hour. Garrett had already done extensive tests that showed driving at this speed caused less vehicle and tire wear, lower frequency and severity of accidents, less driver fatigue, and considerable fuel savings. (Courtesy of the Lawrence Allsberry Estate Collection.)

Multiple crash

An overturned bus blocks the highway in Truckee, Calif., Mon- was one of 13 vehicles involved in a chain-reaction accident during a way. Ten cars and two motorcycles were also involved in the

Even with a great deal of effort towards reducing accidents on the road, some accidents were unavoidable. Although this accident didn't directly involve Garrett Freightlines, it did raise awareness of the possibility of disaster, because a Garrett truck had a similar accident in this area earlier. Noting dangerous stretches of highway and including them in driving reports kept drivers aware of the conditions they could face on particular routes. (Courtesy of the Lawrence Allsberry Estate Collection.)

This particular accident was a grim reminder to all Garrett drivers about the dangers of driving too fast for safety. Although a Garrett driver was involved in this accident, he was not at fault. It was another truck that caused the accident. By following Garrett safe driving regulations, in this case speed, he avoided injury despite being struck by the other truck. One message was made clear in this picture: "Fog+Speed=Trouble." (Courtesy of the Lawrence Allsberry Estate Collection.)

Many Garrett Freightlines truck drivers took pride in their work and dedicated themselves to a mission of safety. This photograph shows three drivers from the Chehalis group. These men were three-fifths of a crew that had worked more than 1,200 days without a personal injury and had gone more than 1,000 days without a vehicle accident. (Courtesy of the Lawrence Allsberry Estate Collection.)

This picture shows a line driver discussing the details of safe driving with Bill Wilson, Garrett Freightlines president in the late 1960s and early 1970s. The hierarchy of the company didn't diminish the importance of communication about safety practices. Managing officials and presidents rarely missed the chance to discuss and learn about better safety practices with lower-level employees. (Courtesy of the Lawrence Allsberry Estate Collection.)

In this photograph, two Garrett Freightlines employees work together to chain up a tire in 1959. The massive pile of chains pictured was likely a common sight at a number of Garrett terminals during the winter months. Garrett wanted to keep a ready supply on hand for trucks and trailers that required chains to function. Tire chains like these were just one example of additional safety equipment provided to Garrett drivers. Inclement weather made driver safety precautions especially critical. (Courtesy of the Lawrence Allsberry Estate Collection.)

Pictured here are the hard-working mechanics in the Garrett shop in Pocatello. The complete records on tires and equipment wear for the Garrett vehicles that operated out of Pocatello were kept by a woman, Mary Brownley. Her meticulous record-keeping facilitated both driver safety and company efficiency, as she provided the Pocatello terminal managers with information about the optimal time to replace worn tires and equipment. After her days of working for Garrett, Brownley went back to school and fulfilled her dream of earning a degree in organ performance from Idaho State University's School of Music. (Courtesy of the Lawrence Allsberry Estate Collection.)

Together with the Idaho State Police, Garrett Freightlines promoted the Lights on for Safety Campaign within the trucking industry. This photograph was taken at the Garrett Terminal in Pocatello as multiple employees and a local policeman inspected the lights on their vehicles to ensure proper functioning. Every part of a tractor and trailer needed to be working properly to ensure a safe trip. (Courtesy of the Steve Port Collection.)

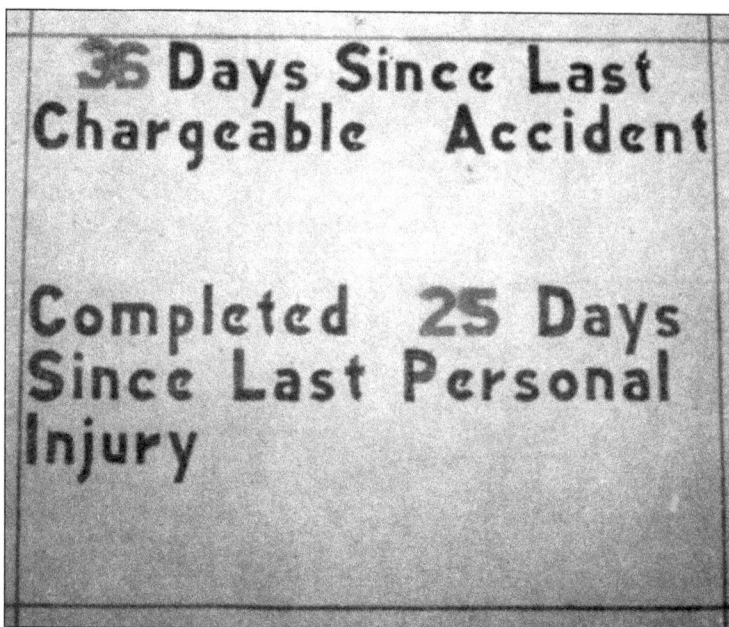

This sign posted at the Ogden terminal in 1969 indicates the terminal's progress on personal injuries and industrial accidents. The Ogden terminal successfully completed the 1968 calendar year without a single personal injury. During 1967–1968, they went 555 days without an injury. (Courtesy of the Lawrence Allsberry Estate Collection.)

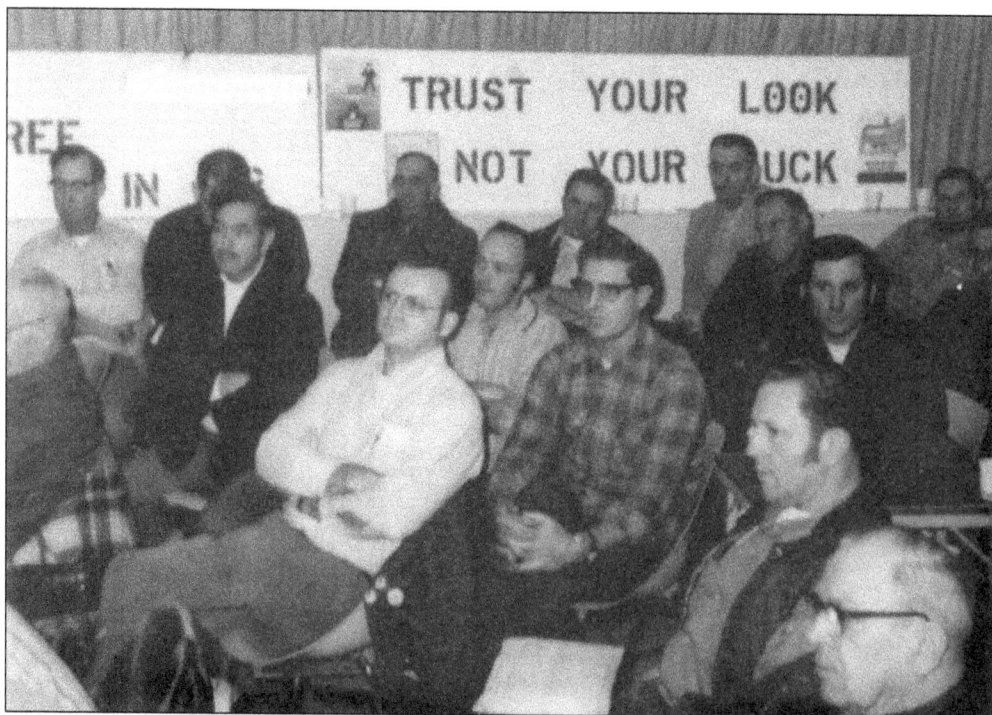

At a Garrett Freightlines safety meeting held in January 1973, drivers were asked to "stay accident free in '73." The drivers pictured are being educated in safety practices to help prevent accidents. Garrett directly placed safety in the control of its employees, as the slogan in the background states: "trust your look, not your luck." (Courtesy of the Lawrence Allsberry Estate Collection.)

Garrett Freightlines made sure to give special recognition to every employee who contributed to the company safety endeavor. Every issue of *Garrett Topics* had lists of employees and their years of safety awards. This was a way to make the employees feel recognized and to encourage their continued safety. This particular safety recognition included a cash reward of $50 as an extra incentive to participate in safe practices. (Courtesy of the Lawrence Allsberry Estate Collection.)

Underscoring the importance that Garrett Freightlines placed on safety, every issue of *Garrett Topics* had at least one page dedicated to awards for safe drivers. Drivers received their first safe-driving award after completing one year without an accident and were subsequently recognized for longer milestones (five years and 10 years without an accident). (Courtesy of the Lawrence Allsberry Estate Collection.)

83

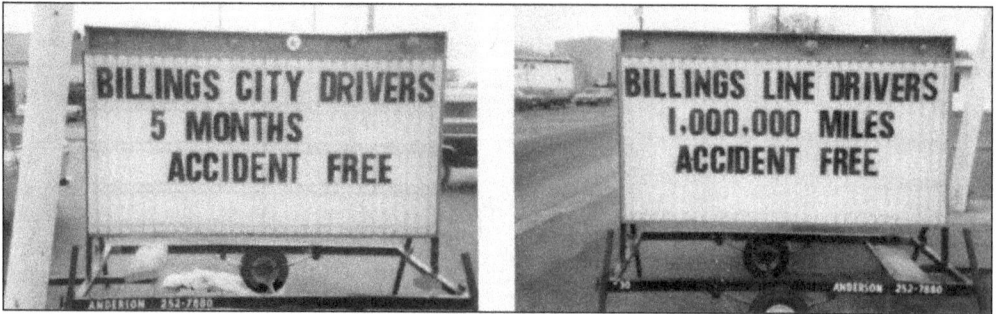

The Garrett terminal in Billings, Montana, proudly displayed a sign on a local street referring to its record and dedication to safety. Meticulous records were kept by Garrett Freightlines concerning individual and terminal safety records, and any opportunity to display outstanding safety performance was welcomed by the employees. Garrett Freightlines encouraged this, as it served as a morale booster and a healthy reminder to all employees and the general community. (Courtesy of the Lawrence Allsberry Estate Collection.)

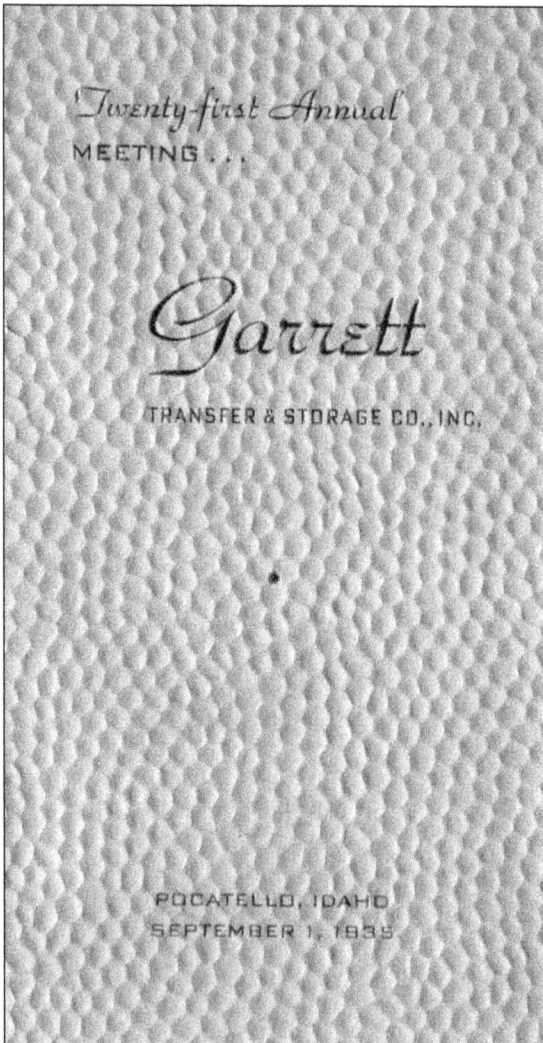

The 21st annual meeting was held on September 1, 1935, in Pocatello; pictured is the program. The itinerary included an "All Employee Meeting," with the first order of business titled "Insurance and Highway Accidents." This proved that even during celebratory events, Garrett Freightlines took opportunities to concentrate on safety awareness. (Courtesy of the Stedtfeld Family Papers, Special Collections, Eli M. Oboler Library, Idaho State University.)

GARRETT FREIGHTLINES, Inc.

P. O. BOX 4048 • POCATELLO, IDAHO • 83201

July 9, 1971

TO ALL TERMINAL MANAGERS

Gentlemen:

We have been awarded the First Place Industrial Safety Placque by the American Trucking Associations, Inc., in the over 2500 employee class for 1970. To win first place means that we had the lowest injury frequency based on man-hours worked and lost-time injuries in the nation. We are real happy about this.

We have made good progress in the reduction of personal injuries and express our gratitude to you for a job well done. As a result of your efforts to reduce personal injuries, we have also received a $290,000. reduction in our insurance premiums from Truck Insurance Exchange.

We can continue to reduce accident costs by showing and telling our employees, in a constructive manner, how to work without an injury.

We are looking forward to receiving first place again this year and further reductions in insurance premiums through our continued efforts.

Congratuations, gentlemen.

MARCUS WOODS
Assistant Director of Safety

MW:hg
cc: B. J. Wilson
     Operations

This letter, written to all terminal managers, informed them about a safety award the company had recently received. This first-place Industrial Safety Award was just one of many awards that Garrett received for its dedication to providing a safe place to work for all employees. The letter also reminds terminal managers to lead by example, something that further exemplifies the company culture and mindset of working together as a family. Ultimately the superior safety in this company came from everyone on the team, from the top management down to the lowest-level employees. Safety was something every employee could be proud of and benefit from, as this helped lower insurance premiums and provided a safe space in which to work. (Courtesy of the Lawrence Allsberry Estate Collection.)

0-76

YEARLY COMPARISON OF INDUSTRIAL INJURIES BY TERMINALS

	1973	1974	1975		1973	1974	1975
Aberdeen	0	1	0				
Albuquerque	2	0	1	Moscow	2	3	3
Anaheim	–	–	2	Moses Lake	2	0	1
Baker	3	2	1	Mount Vernon	2	0	1
Bellingham	1	3	3	Ogden	3	2	1
Billings	19	15	32	Olympia	2	2	0
Boise	21	16	22	Pasco	3	3	6
Bozeman	2	1	0	Payette	2	2	0
Burley	1	3	0	Pendleton	1	0	0
Butte	2	2	1	Pocatello Terminal	32	52	41
Challis	1	0	0	Pocatello Shop	8	10	9
Chehalis	1	0	0	Portland	72	84	71
Cortez	0	0	0	Preston	0	0	1
Denver	59	39	48	Provo	1	1	0
Elko	0	1	0	Reno	8	9	10
Emeryville	26	38	47	Sacramento	9	6	5
Everett	1	1	2	Salmon	0	1	0
Farmington	0	0	1	Salt Lake City	52	32	53
Fresno	2	4	1	San Diego	0	1	0
Glendive	0	3	0	Sandpoint	0	1	0
Grand Junction	0	0	0	San Jose	8	3	5
Great Falls	10	16	8	Seattle	70	70	68
Helena	6	4	3	Shamrock	–	6	5
Idaho Falls	5	5	2	Soda Springs	0	0	0
John Day	0	0	0	Spokane	33	41	32
Kalispell	4	0	3	St. Paul	24	21	17
La Grande	0	1	2	Twin Falls	12	6	6
Las Vegas	2	0	4	Walla Walla	4	5	9
Lewiston	6	1	0	Wheatland	0	0	1
Longview	3	6	6	Yakima	4	7	2
Los Angeles	131	128	119				
Miles City	2	1	0	Totals	676	668	661
Missoula	5	6	6				
Moab	4	2	0				
Montpelier	2	1	0				

This report compares injuries for the past three years in all terminals owned by Garrett. A first glance at the report shows that many of the terminals had fewer than six injuries per year, which is a great reflection of the safety practices in the company. Only a few terminals had large numbers of accidents, with Los Angeles reporting the highest number of incidents. The company had a total of just over 600 accidents for the whole year, yet another indicator of its dedication to safety. (Courtesy of the Lawrence Allsberry Estate Collection.)

Employees received continuous safety training. The four Los Angeles supervisors pictured here spent two weekends attending a front-line supervisor workshop as part of the terminal's efforts to improve operations and safety. The men expressed appreciation for the opportunity to attend the workshop and quickly implemented what they had learned throughout the Los Angeles terminal. (Courtesy of the Lawrence Allsberry Estate Collection.)

Injury	Cost
Carton slipped. Sharp edge tore right thumb	27.00
Co-worker pulled head back causing pinched nerve in neck	80.50
Loading frozens. Wrenched left shoulder	46.00
Loading freight. Severe back strain	81.87 86.14-comp
Vehicular accident. Separated shoulder.	1255.70 1137.50-comp
Vehicular accident. Bruised hip and sprained shoulder	91.23
Vehicular accident. Sprained back, bruised arm, knee and leg	44.59
Vehicular accident. Muscle strain, neck and shoulder	46.00
* * * * * * * * * *	
Cranking landing gear. Handle slipped hitting above left eye, cut and bruised	88.70
Tractor door blew shut hitting top of head. Laceration of scalp.	15.31
Slipped off ladder on truck. Caught hand hold. Pulled ligaments, left arm	48.00
Scratched hand when reaching into sleeper berth. Infected	23.15
Chaining equipment. Caught fingernail. Torn and infected.	14.00
Dolly ran over foot. Smashed toe - had to be lanced.	25.00
Turned pallet jack. Handle flew up hitting above right eye - cut	71.00
Slipped on cab step. Pulled muscles in knee	114.85
Wind blew side panel off flat rack. Back twisted	25.00
Lifting dolly with spare tire on it. Abdominal strain - hernia	

This type of report was created annually to detail every injury occurrence throughout all terminals. This particular report shows a portion of the injuries that took place in the Pocatello terminal. Pocatello had many injuries simply because of its size. However, reading through the lists of injuries, many were very minor. Garrett was committed to tracking and correcting all safety violations and providing for its employees in the event of an accident. (Courtesy of the Lawrence Allsberry Estate Collection.)

Out of the 661 injuries in 1975, most were in the less serious categories of sprains, bruises, and cuts. These types of injuries were common in a setting where heavy equipment and large objects were constantly being moved. (Courtesy of the Lawrence Allsberry Estate Collection.)

PERSONAL INJURIES 1975   661 Injuries

1.	Back - strains, sprains	184	28%
2.	Legs - bruises,cuts, sprains	104	16%
3.	Hands - cuts bruises, broken	77	12%
4	Foot - broken, smashed, sprained	64	10%
5.	Head - cuts, bruises	53	8%
6.	Arm - sprained, cut, bruised	51	7%
8	Shoulder - sprained, bruised	40	6%
9.	Eye - foreign objects	41	6%
10.	Groin - strain	14	2%
11	Ribs, broken, bruised	13	2%
12.	Neck - bruised, sprained	9	1%
13.	Hernia	6	1%
14.	Chest	3	-
15	Heart attacks	2	-

DURING 1975 WE PAID $244,913.86 FOR MEDICAL EXPENSES AND INDEMNITY. KEEP IN MIND WE ARE STILL PAYING ON SOME OF THESE INJURIES AND THE COSTS WILL BE MUCH MORE BEFORE THEY ARE CLOSED.

Gentlemen:

Attached is a recap of on the job personal injuries during 1974 and the total number of injuries by terminal to compare with 1973 injuries.

The alarming part of this recap is the number of lost work day injuries and the number of days lost because of these injuries. With 262 lost work day injuries and a total of 5,243 lost work days means each lost work day injury resulted in 2.3 days away from work per injury. During 1974 all employees worked 6,317,338 man hours with 262 lost work day injuries which results in a figure of 41.47 injuries per million man hours. We must reduce this frequency by 50% during 1975.

To give you a better idea of where we must work the hardest to reduce injuries here is a breakdown by classification.

CLASS	HOURS WORKED	INJURIES	LOST WORK DAYS	FREQUENCY
Line Drivers	2,118,897	36	939	16.99
Local Drivers	1,725,369	105	2,630	60.86
Dock	1,404,079	110	1,361	78.34
Shop	37,513	9	139	239.92
Others	1,031,530	2	165	.19

We ask that you review these injuries with each of your terminals and give us your full support to reduce injuries in 1975.

We provide a safe place for our employees to work and provide good tools for them to do their jobs. Let it be known in all of your terminals that we expect them to do their jobs without injuries.

Gentlemen this is a serious matter and we need your help.

Marcus Woods
MARCUS WOODS
Director of Safety

MW: ath1

The director of safety had an important job: to track and oversee all injuries and accidents within the company. Pictured is a report sent out from the director of safety outlining the injuries in the categories of class, hours worked, injuries, lost workdays, and frequency. The most accident-prone areas were within the terminals, shops, and docking areas. These were often areas of large equipment, moving machinery, and constant reorganization. This report helped demonstrate the distribution of injuries and provide some encouragement to the employees to continue striving for improvement. (Courtesy of the Lawrence Allsberry Estate Collection.)

Safety was important not only for the drivers but for all of Garrett employees. Dock workers often needed to take careful consideration of how they were loading and unloading freight. When lifting heavy items, workers needed to have good form to avoid back injuries and other physical injuries. The equipment and tools they were using could be dangerous as well if not used correctly. Specifically in the hectic dock environment, there were many opportunities for injuries to occur. (Courtesy of the Lawrence Allsberry Estate Collection.)

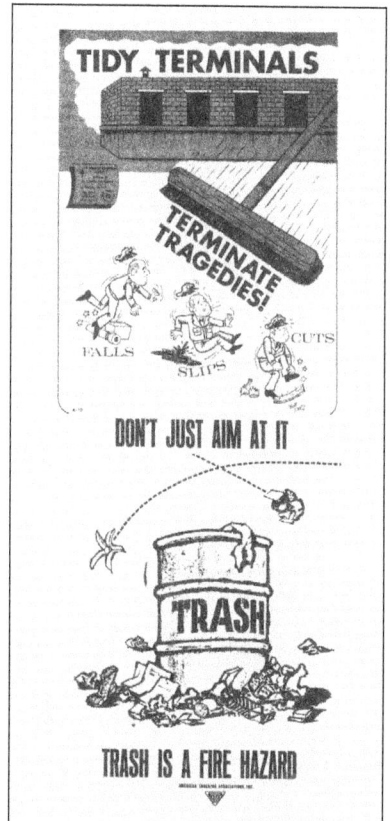

Garrett Topics often printed illustrations promoting the safety values of the company in a fun and lighthearted way. This one shows simple and small ways that everyone could be more safe on the job. Making sure that trash actually gets into the trash cans helps keep the work areas tidy and decreases the risk of injuries. The illustrations were gentle reminders of simple safety precautions all employees should be thinking about. (Courtesy of the Lawrence Allsberry Estate Collection.)

The safety message that Garrett Freightlines preached extended beyond the company to the driving public, since Garrett drivers shared the roads with civilians. This cartoon, "How to be a Good Back Seat Driver," was created by Carol Lane of Shell Oil Company and republished in *Garrett Topics*. (Courtesy of the Lawrence Allsberry Estate Collection.)

"TEN LITTLE DRIVERS"

TEN little drivers, road and weather fine . . . One nodded, fell asleep — then there were nine.

NINE little drivers, one a little late . . . tried to pass upon a hill — so, there were eight.

EIGHT little drivers, one went to heaven . . . He ignored a sign to stop — then there were seven.

SEVEN little drivers, speeding in the sticks . . . Out popped a moving van — now there are only six.

SIX little drivers, laughing and alive . . . One with tires completely bald — skidded, now there's five.

FIVE little drivers, one with faulty door . . . Didn't have his seat belt on — so there's only four.

FOUR little drivers, one who couldn't see . . . with a dirty windshield — that left only three.

THREE little drivers, one of them a "stew" . . . drank a dozen cans of beer — leaving only two.

TWO little drivers, dragging just for fun . . . One didn't see the open ditch — that left only one.

ONE little driver, 'round a curve he tore . . . lost control and hit a tree — there isn't any more.

Poems and cartoons concerning safety were commonly published in *Garrett Topics*. Many of the materials were composed and submitted by employees within the company, although the authors are now unknown. The cartoon below looks like the original "Grumpy Cat" and humorously communicates a serious message about the problem of carelessness. This is just another example of how Garrett Freightlines strived to keep safety at the forefront of all of its employees' minds. (Both, courtesy of the Lawrence Allsberry Estate Collection.)

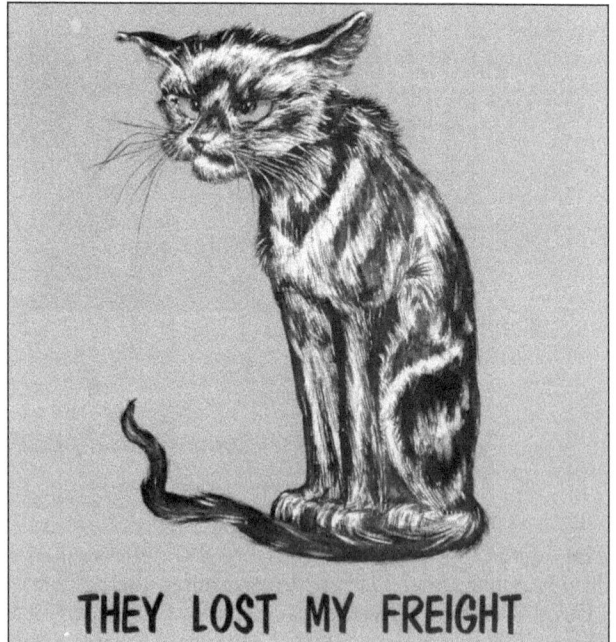

THEY LOST MY FREIGHT

Six

TAKEOVER ATTEMPTS AND LABOR MOVEMENTS

Part of building Garrett Freightlines included developing marketing techniques to promote and further advance the growth of the company. Appearing on various memorabilia are catchy phrases such as "We Do Care," "Excellence of Service," and "The Carrier with Careabilty," used by employees, existing customers, and new prospective customers but also drawing attention from both local and national competitors alike.

Garrett Freightlines was a cash-rich and prosperous company, becoming a prime candidate for hostile takeovers by other trucking companies that sought to acquire Garrett in hopes of gaining substantial market share in the transportation industry. A rival company, Navajo Freight Lines, attempted to take control of Garrett Freightlines by purchasing stock from some of Garrett's stockholders and exercising voting rights to elect individuals to the board of directors. The tactics through which Navajo sought to gain control of Garrett led to a series of lawsuits over several years in the 1960s and into the 1970s. In the end, Garrett Freightlines prevailed in its attempt to safeguard a beloved company that instilled pride and loyalty in its employees.

Throughout its history, Garrett withstood many challenges and knew the importance of taking care of employees who were regarded almost as family. As American labor unions started gaining increasing power in the trucking industry, employees from Garrett Freightlines joined the International Brotherhood of Teamsters. Garrett's leadership participated in negotiations as Teamsters representatives sought a series of reforms centered on better wages, benefits, working conditions, and handling of disputes over violations of contract revisions. For top managers at freight carriers throughout the western United States, negotiating with the Teamsters meant sitting across the table from Jimmy Hoffa.

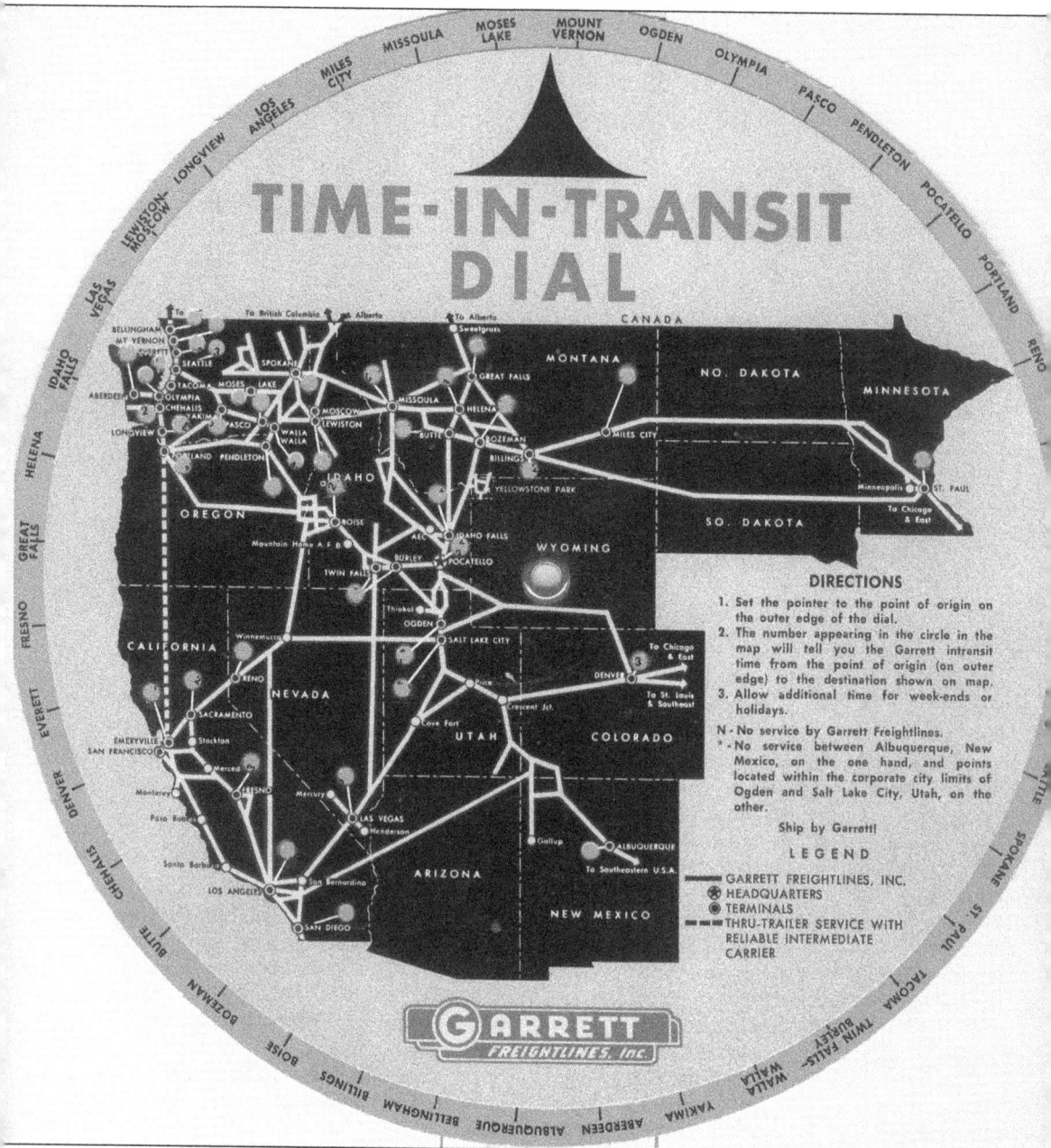

Beginning in the 1950s, Garrett Freightlines developed useful marketing devices to promote and add value to the company. The device shown here, a manual "time-in-transit" dial, allowed customers to spin the top layer until an arrow pointed to the origin of their shipment. The map below would then tell the number of days the transportation would take to reach various destination cities. (Courtesy of the Lawrence Allsberry Estate Collection.)

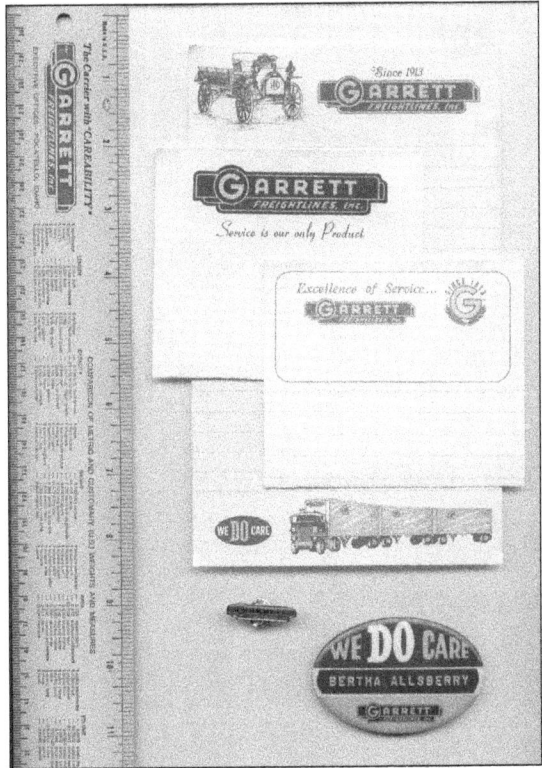

Garrett Freightlines incorporated various marketing materials embossed with the company's logo and motto. These were given to employees, existing customers, and prospective customers to promote the Garrett brand. Garrett Freightlines was a good early example of a company in the transportation industry that developed a brand with a consistent look and feel. This drew attention to Garrett from potential new customers, but it also attracted attention from rival companies who had an interest in a hostile takeover bid. (Right, courtesy of the William Q. McNeil Collection, Special Collections, Eli M. Oboler Library, Idaho State University; below, courtesy of the Lawrence Allsberry Estate Collection.)

As part of the continual marketing and brand recognition efforts, drivers were armed with business cards to help connect with others who sought transportation services provided by Garrett Freightlines. Furthermore, all drivers had uniforms embossed with the company's logo to help set them apart and make them representatives for Garrett Freightlines. (Courtesy of the Jack Wenske Collection, Special Collections, Eli M. Oboler Library, Idaho State University.)

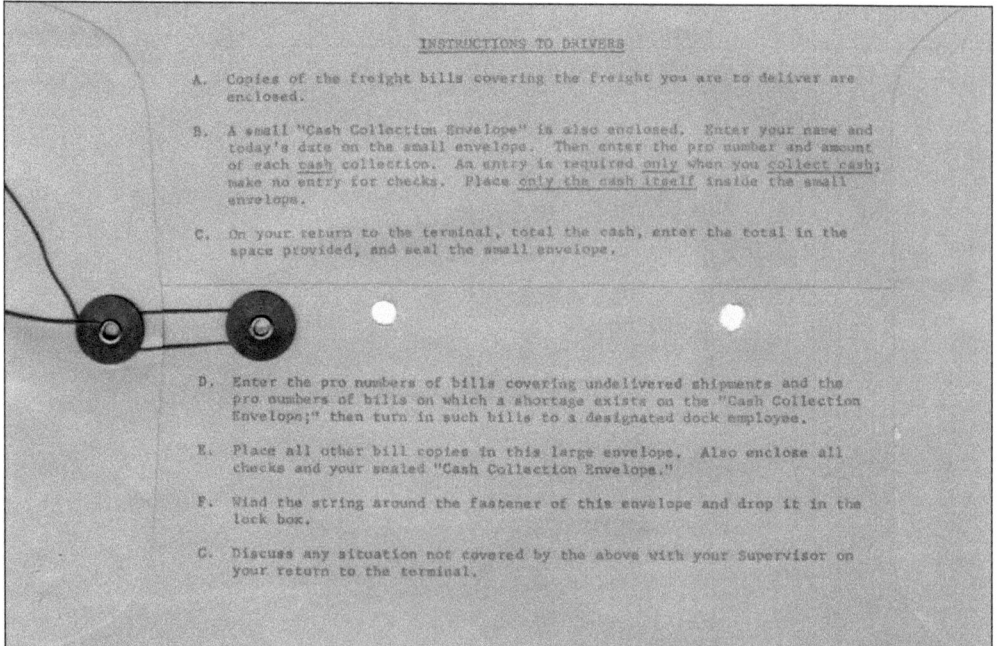

INSTRUCTIONS TO DRIVERS

A. Copies of the freight bills covering the freight you are to deliver are enclosed.

B. A small "Cash Collection Envelope" is also enclosed. Enter your name and today's date on the small envelope. Then enter the pro number and amount of each cash collection. An entry is required only when you collect cash; make no entry for checks. Place only the cash itself inside the small envelope.

C. On your return to the terminal, total the cash, enter the total in the space provided, and seal the small envelope.

D. Enter the pro numbers of bills covering undelivered shipments and the pro numbers of bills on which a shortage exists on the "Cash Collection Envelope;" then turn in such bills to a designated dock employee.

E. Place all other bill copies in this large envelope. Also enclose all checks and your sealed "Cash Collection Envelope."

F. Wind the string around the fastener of this envelope and drop it in the lock box.

G. Discuss any situation not covered by the above with your Supervisor on your return to the terminal.

One of the responsibilities of a Garrett truck driver was to collect cash upon delivery. This cash collection envelope provides instructions to drivers on how to collect delivery freight bills. Clarence Garrett instilled a careful cash management strategy emphasizing cash collections, paying bills within 10 days of receipt, and accumulating cash discounts rather than paying with credit. The company's conservative financial practices and robust cash position contributed to its attractiveness as a candidate for hostile takeovers. (Courtesy of the Lawrence Allsberry Estate Collection.)

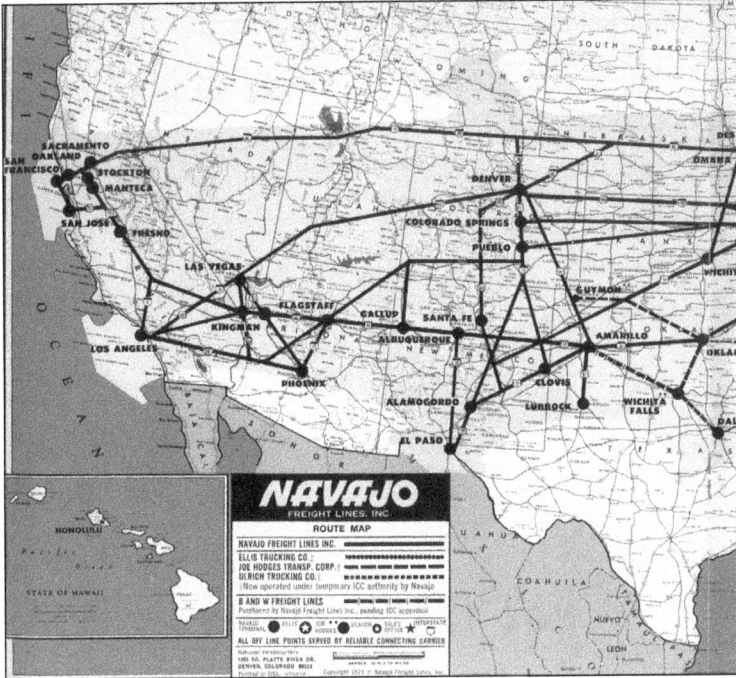

Garrett Freightlines became a prime target for an attempted takeover by Navajo Freight Lines for many reasons. The company had large cash holdings, well-known safety practices, an experienced and loyal community of workers, and a multitude of routes. In 1968, Garrett had over $51 million in revenue, $11 million more than Navajo Freight Lines. Merging the two companies would have resulted in a 58.7-percent market share of the trucking industry from Denver to Las Vegas and a 42.4-percent market share from the San Francisco Bay Area to Denver. The map above shows the routes of Navajo Freight Lines, and the image below displays the routes of Garrett Freightlines. By gaining control of both routes, Navajo would have substantially decreased competition, resulting in a great deal of control over the industry. (Both, courtesy of the Stedtfeld Family Papers, Special Collections, Eli M. Oboler Library, Idaho State University.)

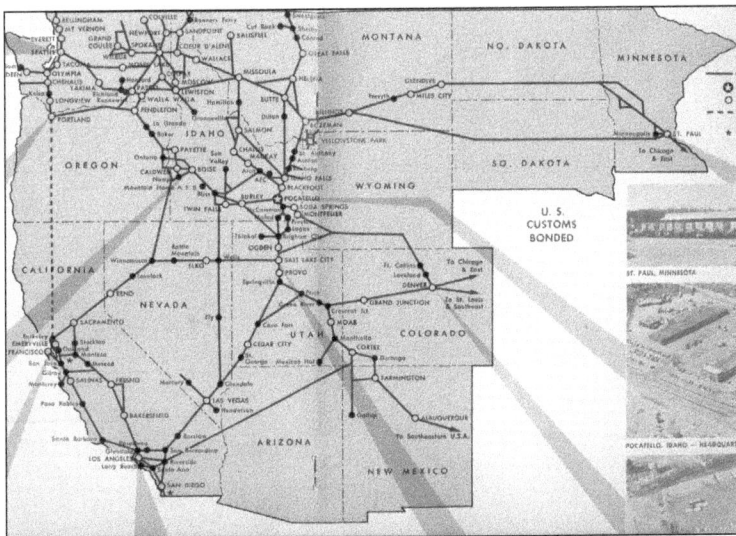

This collateral receipt from 1971 shows that Navajo Freight Lines acquired 2,748 shares, or 27.9 percent of Garrett Freightlines stock. This prompted several lawsuits involving claimed antitrust and securities law violations and ultimately proceedings before the ICC concerning unlawful control of Garrett by Navajo. In 1970, Garrett formally filed a lawsuit. Navajo countered with a suit of its own, only to drop the charges within the year. (Courtesy of the Stedtfeld Family Papers, Special Collections, Eli M. Oboler Library, Idaho State University.)

Recd. 10-31-70

UNITED STATES DEPARTMENT OF JUSTICE

WASHINGTON, D.C. 20530

Address Reply to the
Division Indicated
and Refer to Initials and Number

RWMcL:JJS:LLC
60-0-38-61

October 28, 1970

REGISTERED MAIL
RETURN RECEIPT REQUESTED

Mr. Norman V. Stedtfeld
155 South 19 Avenue
Pocatello, Idaho 83201

Dear Mr. Stedtfeld:

The Federal Bureau of Investigation has advised us that, in order to supply us with certain requested information relating to negotiations and transactions conducted between you and Navajo Freight Lines or other related companies or individuals, you desire to have the questions submitted to you in writing. Accordingly, we are communicating with you directly rather than causing additional expenditure of FBI investigative effort.

The questions submitted for your response are:

1. How much stock of Garrett Freightlines, Inc. did you own in 1965?

2. How much stock of Garrett do you presently own?

3. Have you made any acquisitions of Garrett stock in the period 1965 to present?

4. Have you sold any or all of your holdings in Garrett?

5. At any time since 1965, has one or more offers been made to purchase your shares of Garrett?

6. Describe in detail the negotiations leading to each such offer, including

    a. who initiated the negotiations leading to each such offer,

The US Department of Justice initiated an investigation into the relations of Navajo Freight Lines and Garrett Freightlines on October 28, 1970. In this correspondence, questions were submitted for response from Garrett, which requested them in writing rather than speaking directly with the FBI. (Courtesy of the Stedtfeld Family Papers, Special Collections, Eli M. Oboler Library, Idaho State University.)

Navajo, a motor common carrier of general commodities with routes from Los Angeles and San Francisco to Fort Wayne, Indiana, had control of several other carriers through stock ownership. Two of these were Navajo Freight Lines, a New Mexico corporation, and Navajo Terminals, an Indiana corporation. Navajo Freight Lines was in turn controlled by United Transportation Investment Company out of Chicago, which owned 90 percent of Navajo's capital stock. Navajo Freight Lines owned 1,700 shares of common stock in Garrett Freightlines, and Navajo Terminals owned 143,895 shares. (Courtesy of the Stedtfeld Family Papers, Special Collections, Eli M. Oboler Library, Idaho State University.)

June 23, 1971

Mr. Norman V. Stedtfeld
155 South 19th Avenue
Pocatello, Idaho

Dear Mr. Stedfeld:

Attached you will find the "Certificate of Resolution" and "Irrevocable Stock Power" of Navajo Terminals, Inc. authorizing the transfer of the voting trust certificates representing 5,496 shares of Garrett Freightlines, Inc. common stock to Navajo Freight Lines, Inc. Also, attached is a letter to Mr. Robert Pence of the Idaho First National Bank, which you may sign and forward for authorizing the above transfer. We would appreciate it if you would forward our copy to us when this is accomplished.

By this letter Navajo Freight Lines, Inc. hereby consents to the pledging of the voting trust certificates representing 5,496 shares of Garrett Freightlines, Inc. common stock in escrow as security for the debt to Norman V. Stedtfeld as evidenced by the promissary note dated November 26, 1969, of our wholly-owned subsidiary, Navajo Terminals, Inc.

Thank you in advance for your cooperation in this matter.

Very truly yours,

NAVAJO FREIGHT LINES, INC.

L. F. Mattingley
Executive Vice President

gk

Enclosure

Navajo Freight Lines issued this official letter to Garrett Freightlines as a means to end a long, hard fight between the two companies. As a result, Navajo Freight Lines transferred 5,496 shares of Garrett Freightlines common stock owned by one of its subsidiaries back to Garrett Freightlines, reinstating ownership and preserving the company's headquarters in Pocatello. (Courtesy of the Stedtfeld Family Papers, Special Collections, Eli M. Oboler Library, Idaho State University.)

F. I. duPONT, GLORE FORGAN & CO.   **IRREVOCABLE STOCK OR BOND POW**

FOR VALUE RECEIVED, the undersigned does (do) hereby sell, assign and transfer to

Navajo Freight Lines, Inc.

1205 South Platte River Drive

Denver, Colorado 80223

Voting Trust Certificates representing

IF STOCK, COMPLETE THIS PORTION 5,496 shares of the Common stock of Garrett Freightlines, Inc.

represented by Certificate(s) No(s). _____ inclusive,

standing in the name of the undersigned on the books of said Company.

IF BONDS, COMPLETE THIS PORTION _____ bonds of _____

in the principal amount of $_____, No(s). _____ inclusive,

standing in the name of the undersigned on the books of said Company.

The undersigned does (do) hereby irrevocably constitute and appoint Idaho First

National Bank _____ attorney to transfer the said ~~xxxxxxxxxxxxxxxxxxxxxxxxxxxxxxxxx~~ Voting Trust Certificates on

the books of said Company, with full power of substitution in the premises.

Dated June 25, 1971

David H. Ratner (signature)

IMPORTANT – READ CAREFULLY

The signature(s) to this Power must correspond with the name(s) as written upon the face of the certificate(s) or bond(s) in every particular without alteration or enlargement or any change whatever. Signature guarantee should be made by a member or member organization of the New York Stock Exchange, members of other Exchanges having signatures on file with transfer agent or by a commercial bank or trust company having its principal office or correspondent in the City of New York.

David H. Ratner, President

(PERSON(S) EXECUTING THIS POWER SIGN(S) HERE)

Navajo Terminals, Inc.

F I D 1084 (10-70)

ACCOUNT NUMBER			
OFF.	ACCT	T	A/

This image of an irrevocable stock or bond power complements the concession letter issued by Navajo Freight Lines, proving that it upheld its word and returned Garrett's stock on June 25, 1971. The form is signed by David H. Ratner, president of Navajo Terminals Inc. (Courtesy of the Stedtfeld Family Papers, Special Collections, Eli M. Oboler Library, Idaho State University.)

In July 1971, Garrett formally requested the ICC to deny Navajo's application for control of Garrett Freightlines as the companies were in direct competition since 1965. Garrett cited this as harassment and intimidation and indicated that a takeover would threaten Garrett's philosophy of serving both small and large communities. This photograph shows the 1973 retirement celebration for Maurey Greene (second from the left, to the right of Larry Allsberry and to the left of Bill Wilson), a lead attorney in arguing Garrett's case successfully before the ICC. (Courtesy of the Lawrence Allsberry Estate Collection.)

Garrett vs. Navajo

Garrett Freightlines of Pocatello has received a favorable Report and Order from the Interstate Commerce Commission in Garrett's efforts to stop a take-over attempt by Navajo Freightlines of Denver, Colorado. The 48-page decision by the full Commission (one commissioner dissenting in part and one not participating) essentially affirmed the recommendations in the Initial Decision issued by an Administrative Law Judge of the Commission in January, 1975, but differed as to some of his findings.

The Commission agreed with the Administrative Law Judge that Navajo failed to control Garrett Freightlines in violation of the Interstate Commerce Act and denied Navajo's application for authority to acquire control of Garrett for the reason that it has not been shown to be consistent with the public interest.

The Report and Order also found Navajo's acquisition of Garrett stock to be a violation of the Clayton Anti-Trust Act and ordered Navajo to divest itself of Garrett stock within four years of the effective date of the Order. The Initial Decision by the Administrative Law Judge had recommended a one year period for divestiture.

Also the Commission affirmed the Administrative Law Judge's recommendation that the voting trust proposal by Navajo was insufficient to settle the proceedings, however, ordered Navajo to place all Garrett stock owned by it in its proposed voting trust for the four year period or until full divestiture is accomplished.

The Commission Report and Order was served May 5, 1976 and was to be effective thirty-five days from that date. On June 2, 1976, Navajo requested an extension of time to file a Petition for reconsideration of the Report and Order which the Commission granted to Aug. 3, 1976. Other parties may reply to the Petition by Aug. 23, 1976, with the effective date of the Order postponed pending disposition of the Petition.

The Commission issued its decision after nearly ten years of maneuvering by Navajo to take-over Garrett and legal disputes including four separate court cases and the present Commission proceedings. The Interstate Commerce Commission instituted its investigation into alleged unlawful control of Garrett by Navajo in 1970 including possible antitrust violations. Navajo countered by filing an application to acquire control of Garrett and proposed a voting trust in settlement of the Commission investigation. Purchases by Navajo of Garrett stock began in 1965, over eleven years ago. ⓖ

Featured in the July 1976 issue of *Garrett Topics*, this article informed Garrett's employees of the latest happenings with Navajo Freight Lines. It boasted of a favorable decision made by the ICC ridding Garrett of an 11-year battle against Navajo Freight Lines attempting to take over the company through illegally acquiring Garrett's stock. However, Navajo filed for an extension to petition for reconsideration. Navajo's application for control of Garrett was denied as it was not in the public interest, but Navajo was also not found guilty of all the charges it faced because of its inability to gain control of Garrett Freightlines. (Courtesy of the Lawrence Allsberry Estate Collection.)

Garrett Freightlines trucks and trailers sit in their terminal, idled. A national lockout grounded thousands of trucks and long-haul trailers during a labor dispute in 1967. Garrett Freightlines ceased trucking operations in honor of a nationwide shutdown in retaliation for wildcat strikes by the Teamsters Union. It was reported that crew members and management personnel were out of work and left in the office to man the phones. (Courtesy of the Richard J. Heinz Collection, Special Collections, Eli M. Oboler Library, Idaho State University.)

"Lock 'er up" was heard across the nation. Behind padlocked gates, trucks and trailer boxes stood idle as 65 percent of the US long-distance trucking operations shut down. Hundreds of the nation's trucking firms joined the lockout. As negotiations took place, many union workers agreed that the tie-up would have a detrimental effect upon the nation's economy. It was estimated that $300 million was ultimately lost in potential sales and income. (Courtesy of the Jack Wenske Collection, Special Collections, Eli M. Oboler Library, Idaho State University.)

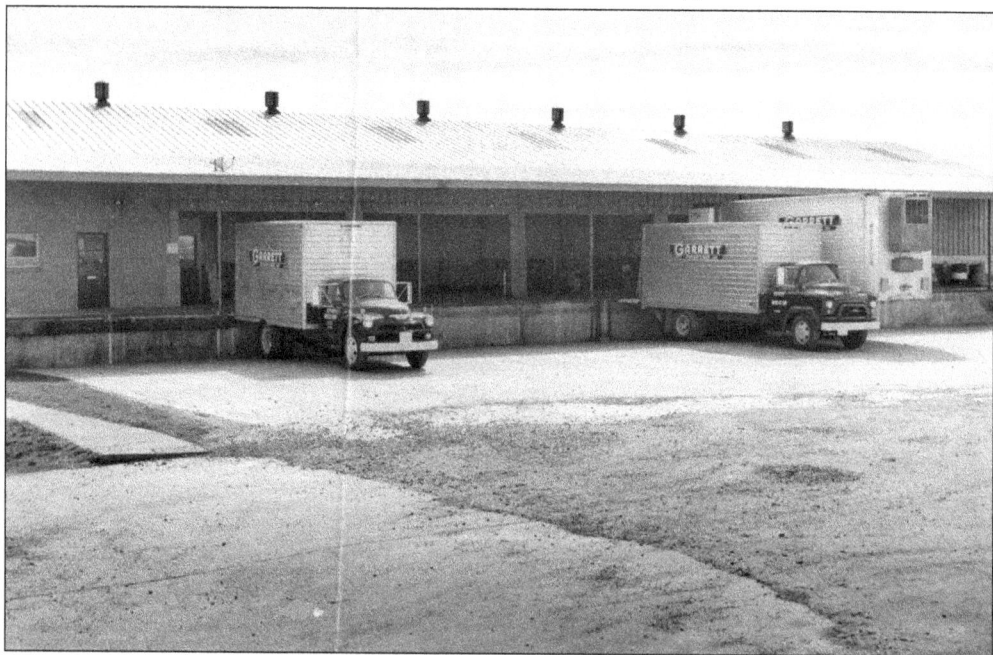

All is quiet at local terminals. Trucking employers and the Teamsters Union were unable to reach an agreement on the new contract terms. In 1967, the average trucker's wage ranged from $3.25 to $5 an hour. (Courtesy of the Jack Wenske Collection, Special Collections, Eli M. Oboler Library, Idaho State University.)

Pickets go up nationwide at Garrett Freightlines as men ask for a fair settlement. The last trucks to move and haul shipment were those dispatched prior to midnight, leaving supervisory personnel to load and unload the "Trailer-Train." It was reported that the Teamsters ordered a lockout because they were intent upon creating a crisis in order to pressure Lyndon Johnson's administration into seeking a Taft-Hartley (back-to-work) injunction. (Courtesy of *Idaho State Journal*.)

NEW YORK WASHINGTON

Analysis

52

The Taft-Hartley Labor Law

—Its Effect On Your Labor Relations—

*Research Institute
of America*
*292 Madison Avenue
New York 17, N.Y.*

In 1947, a law known as the Taft-Hartley Act was passed by Congress prohibiting a list of "unfair" labor practices and restrictions of labor unions. As the national lockout developed, government officials became concerned with the simultaneous trucking shutdowns that could have severe effects on the nation's economy. However, the strike did not appear to warrant a finding of peril to the nation's health and safety, which would have triggered an 80-day cooling-off injunction by the government under the Taft-Hartley law. (Courtesy of the Stedtfeld Family Papers, Special Collections, Eli M. Oboler Library, Idaho State University.)

In April 1967, a settlement was reached between the Teamsters Union and Garrett Freightlines. Garrett Freightlines had 2,600 employees, of which 200 were Teamsters in the local region. The proposed contract included an estimated 50¢ wage hike, cost-of-living pay increases, higher pension and health benefits, and an increase in per-mile payment to long-haul drivers. Responsibility for implementing the contract fell to Bill Wilson (pictured here with a replica of "Rosie the Reo"), who took over as company president following Clarence Garrett's passing. (Courtesy of the Lawrence Allsberry Estate Collection.)

Jimmy Hoffa, president of the Teamsters Union from 1958 until 1971, helped secure a first labor agreement in 1964 and played a role in growing the 1.8 million union memberships. He became involved with organized crime and subscribed to the philosophy "Take care of your friends and whip your enemies." Larry Allsberry, then the vice president of operations for Garrett Freightlines, told the story of an unpleasant experience negotiating with Jimmy Hoffa and other Teamsters representatives while serving on the collective bargaining committee for the American Trucking Association in the late 1960s. Hoffa disappeared in 1975 and was ultimately declared deceased. (Courtesy of International Brotherhood of Teamsters Local No. 983.)

Seven

THE FALL AND LEGACY OF GARRETT FREIGHTLINES

Clarence Garrett died unexpectedly in 1967. Although new management took over, the company had lost its founder and visionary, and the effects were felt companywide. Over the next decade, the company navigated many changes to the trucking industry that contributed to Garrett's dissolution. Deregulation fundamentally altered the competitive dynamics among freight carriers. Trade routes that gave Garrett Freightlines its regional competitive advantage were suddenly made readily available to any company that was willing and able to take them. The company culture and experimental equipment on which Garrett Freightlines prided itself was lost as focus shifted toward narrowing profit margins.

The end of Garrett Freightlines' prominence was marked by its purchase from Dyson-Kissner Corporation by American Natural Resources (ANR) at the close of the 1970s. So too went the local terminals, original logo, and company culture. The expansion strategies of ANR pushed Garrett beyond its capabilities, and the original terminal in Pocatello closed in 1985. Nonetheless, even today, more than three decades after leaving, Garrett Freightlines is still remembered by the citizens of Pocatello, and the original Garrett logo can still be seen throughout town.

Vince Davis (left) and Clarence Garrett show off the original Reo truck used by Garrett Freightlines to patrons of the Idaho State Fair. Shortly after this picture was taken, Clarence Garrett's unexpected death left his company in turmoil. He died without a will, and as those who would lay claim to his business and inheritance battled, company morale suffered. (Courtesy of the Lawrence Allsberry Estate Collection.)

Following the death of Clarence Garrett in 1967, longtime right-hand man Bill Wilson took the reins as the new Garrett Freightlines president. Possessing the same "job comes first" attitude as his predecessor and mentor, Wilson encouraged employees to get back to work and focus on the future of the company rather than dwelling on the death of their founder and longtime president. (Courtesy of the Lawrence Allsberry Estate Collection.)

A replica of the original 1913 Reo truck, a profound symbol of the company that by the 1970s had become known as the "Gatehouse Lady," is shown in this photograph being taken down off the Gatehouse for repair and restoration work. This symbol still stands on the Gatehouse today as a memory of what Garrett Freightlines, and the Pocatello community, was built upon. (Courtesy of the Lawrence Allsberry Estate Collection.)

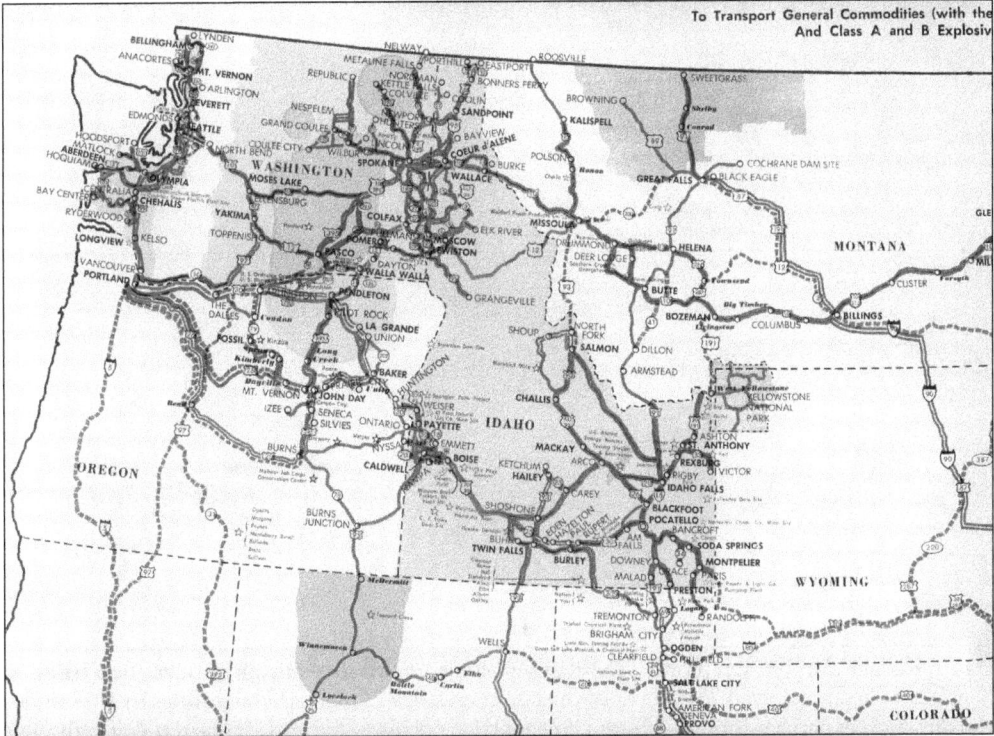

This map shows the extensive web of shipping routes to which Garrett Freightlines owned rights in the West. The ability to ship throughout 13 states was one of Garrett's most valuable assets and the reason the company fought so hard to prevent legislation that would deregulate the trucking industry. (Courtesy of the Lawrence Allsberry Estate Collection.)

Garrett Freightlines president Larry Allsberry presided over the company during a time of major changes to US freight industry regulations. Deregulation brought with it major concerns for Garrett, as the company had spent years obtaining the rights to valuable trucking routes throughout the western United States. (Courtesy of the *Idaho State Journal*.)

Photo by Jerry Gillette on New Year's Day during early stages of construction.

Dyson-Kissner Corporation (now Dyson-Kissner-Moran), a private equity investment firm based in New York City, purchased 78 percent of the common stock of Garrett Freightlines in 1977 under the direction of partner John A. Moran. At that time nothing changed for Garrett culturally, but the community was worried that the new owners would take the Garrett headquarters outside of Pocatello. Instead, Moran stated that his goals were to keep the headquarters in Pocatello and to establish an Idaho State University scholarship for Garrett children in memory of Clarence Garrett. (Courtesy of the Lawrence Allsberry Estate Collection.)

THE DYSON-KISSNER CORPORATION

230 Park Avenue
New York, New York 10017
(212) 661-4600

One Washington Mall
Boston, Massachusetts 02108
(617) 723-3513

Officers

John A. Moran	President
Bushrod W. Burns, Jr.	Vice President
James A. McLean	Vice President
Brian D. Murphy	Vice President
Ralph L. Shapcott	Vice President
Robert L. Wallace	Vice President
Henry C. Ulrichs	Treasurer
Joseph M. Dunn	Controller
Charles H. Dyson	Chairman of the Board
Franklin H. Kissner	Director

In October 1978, talks were underway for American Natural Resources, an oil and gas corporation with growing holdings in the transportation industry, to purchase Garrett Freightlines from Dyson-Kissner Corporation. The final sale was completed on August 7, 1979, exchanging Garrett Freightlines for 900,000 shares of ANR stock. ANR was a conglomerate, and purchasing Garrett allowed ANR to hold a portfolio of truck lines with authority to operate across the United States from coast to coast. (Courtesy of the Lawrence Allsberry Estate Collection.)

Interest in ANR's purchase of Garrett Freightlines was intense in Pocatello, because local residents feared that ANR would move the company's headquarters to a larger metropolitan area. In this photograph, Garrett president Larry Allsberry and ANR chief executive officer Arthur Seder sit down for interviews with local print and broadcast media. The representatives from ANR were later treated to a formal reception at the Pocatello Hilton. (Courtesy of the Lawrence Allsberry Estate Collection.)

Following ANR's purchase, the famous Garrett Freightlines logo, a large capital "G" in green-and-gold lettering, was replaced with a red, white, and blue color scheme. However, the original logo can still be found throughout Pocatello and on the many pieces of memorabilia scattered among former employees and Garrett enthusiasts. (Courtesy of the Lawrence Allsberry Estate Collection.)

116

The original letterhead (above) shows the bold Garrett letters in green and gold and the well-loved "G." The rebranded letterhead (below) was used after the company merged with ANR. It has a rainbow outline of the United States and bold Garrett lettering on top. (Both, courtesy of the Lawrence Allsberry Estate Collection.)

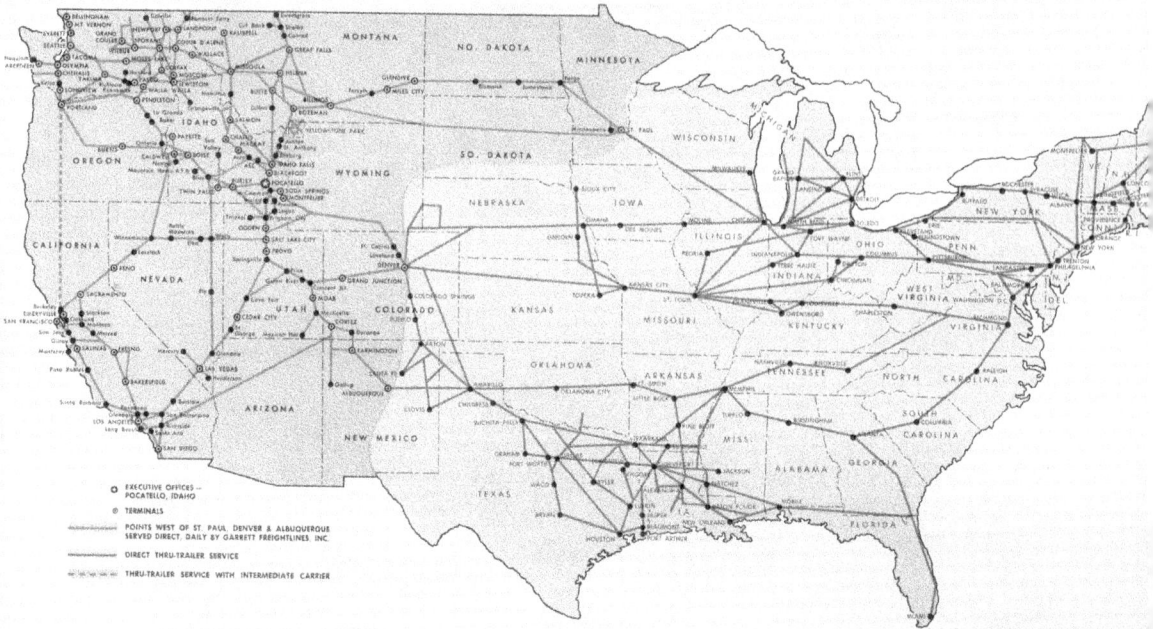

DEPENDABLE TRANSPORTATION ACROSS THE NATION!

TRANSCONTINENTAL SERVICE THROUGH THREE STRATEGIC GATEWAYS

A Northern Route
Minneapolis and St. Paul connect the Great Northwest with the industrial areas of the Great Lakes and Northeast U.S.A.

A Central Route
Denver connects the entire West with the Midwest, Eastern, and Southwestern markets.

A Southern Route
Albuquerque connects the West and Northwest with the Industrial Southeast.

When Garrett was purchased, ANR's strategy was to expand the truck routes to increase the company's reach. This photograph shows a map of the planned expansion, which would provide northern, central, and southern transportation routes from coast to coast. Consolidating regional carriers into a single unit with authority from the federal government to haul freight cross-country offered a prospective competitive advantage while the trucking industry was regulated. However, the growing deregulation of the industry under the Reagan administration eroded the advantages of that strategy. (Courtesy of the Lawrence Allsberry Estate Collection.)

This foldout advertised a move Garrett made under ANR to maintain a top position in commercial transportation. Due to a rise in long-distance travel costs associated with trucking and the cheaper cost of long-distance travel by train, ANR-Garrett encouraged companies to use Garrett Freightlines' services to transport goods to and from local train stops. (Courtesy of the Lawrence Allsberry Estate Collection.)

INTRODUCING ValuLINER SERVICE

THE SENSIBLE WAY TO MOVE GOODS ACROSS AMERICA!

IDAHO STATE JOURNAL

WEATHER
Details on Page A-

Snow

VOL. LXXVII NO. 254   POCATELLO, IDAHO   TUESDAY, JANUARY 8, 1985   25 CENTS

© Copyright, 1985, Idaho State Publishing Co. All rights reserved

arrett's Office to Leave Pocatell

On January 8, 1985, a headline in the local newspaper confirmed that Garrett Freightlines would be leaving the Pocatello area after nearly 72 years of operation. Upon the closing of the Pocatello terminal, former Garrett employees were given the option of relocating to the Salt Lake City terminal or unemployment. Closing a major employer like Garrett was a big blow to Pocatello's economy. (Courtesy of the *Idaho State Journal*.)

This photograph shows one of the vintage Garrett outfits on which mechanics such as Bob Pierce, who with his wife, Jeannie, sat down for an interview with students in 2015, labored tirelessly. Bob worked as a Garrett mechanic from 1950 until 1985, when he was asked by ANR to relocate to the Salt Lake City terminal. Both Bob and Jeannie speak fondly of Garrett Freightlines, referring to the company as their "second family" and lamenting the loss of one of Pocatello's oldest major employers. (Courtesy of the Lawrence Allsberry Estate Collection.)

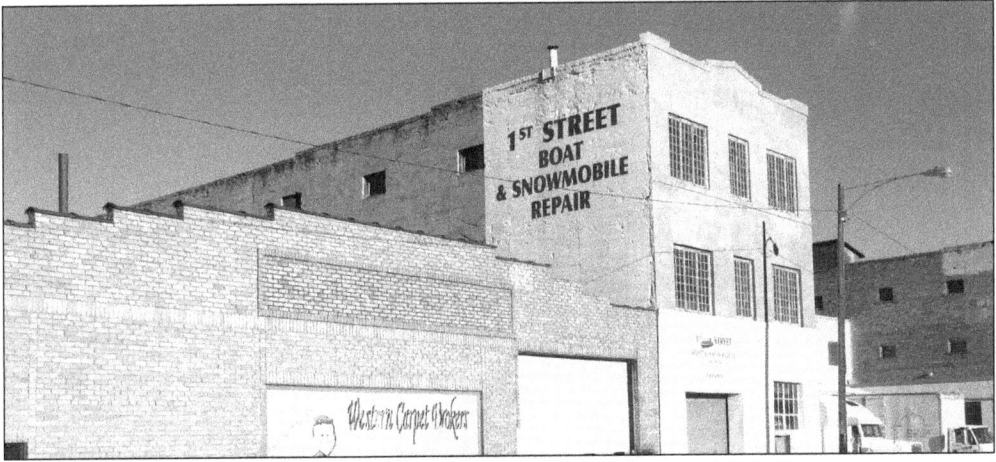

The original Garrett shipping terminal from 1913 is shown here in 2015. Close examination of the photograph shows the fading lettering on the brick exterior reading "Garrett." Across the street from this terminal is the old Union Pacific terminal. Garrett's proximity to the train station played a critical role in the company's ability to fulfill the goal of a 24-hour shipping promise. (Courtesy of Doug Chambers.)

An abandoned Garrett shipping container, with the fading promotion of its once-innovative refrigeration service, sits corroding in the mountains east of Pocatello. This deteriorating relic serves as a poignant reminder of the once-vibrant and thriving company, a major player in the transportation industry of the United States but now hidden from the public eye and slowly fading from memory. (Courtesy of Gabe Flicker Photography.)

The Garrett legacy lives on even as new businesses move into the old Garrett Freightlines spaces. The buildings now house government offices, a school, and a plumbing supply store, as well as modern trucking companies. Every inch of the old buildings is being used in new ways today. (Courtesy of Rich Kirkland of Dale's Inc. Commercial Real Estate Services.)

This symbol of Garrett Freightlines, the famed Gatehouse Lady, has a particularly interesting back story. This truck was found in pieces at Idaho State University, where it was traded for a vintage diesel engine and put back together. The restored vehicle was placed on top of the Gatehouse at its old home. (Courtesy of Rich Kirkland of Dale's Inc. Commercial Real Estate Services.)

This is the remodeled original Garrett Freightlines truck. It is kept out of harm's way in the lobby of the former shop at the Garrett Freightlines property on Garrett Way in Pocatello. This truck has been refurbished to resemble the original and to last many more generations. (Courtesy of Rich Kirkland of Dale's Inc. Commercial Real Estate Services.)

This is one of the many loading bays on the old Garrett Freightlines property. The bay in the back has held many things, including human organs at one time. These organs were being transported between donors and recipients, sometimes across many states, to save lives. (Courtesy of Rich Kirkland of Dale's Inc. Commercial Real Estate Services.)

The street that grew in front of the newer Garrett buildings and that connects the western edge of Pocatello to Interstate 86 is now known as Garrett Way. This road is a major route across the city for locals, and is also a primary throughway for commercial transportation. (Courtesy of Chelsea Kavanaugh.)

Bob Garrett, nephew of Clarence Garrett, is shown holding a picture of the first tractor and trailer he ever drove, a 1946 Kenworth tractor with a 40-foot trailer. Bob started working with Garrett in 1946 at age 14 and continued with the company until the final days. (Courtesy of Lisa Cecil.)

In the end, the enduring culture of Garrett Freightlines is still safely protected by those who responded to the challenge of sustaining safety within the company. Some of the company's advertising campaigns may seem dated, clichéd, or out of step with contemporary sensibilities. What time cannot dull is the enormity of what Garrett Freightlines accomplished, its important contributions to the development of the trucking industry in America, and its positive impact on

Pocatello and communities throughout the western United States. The Garrett legacy is one of trying new ideas and finding better ways, conveying the importance of safety and reliability, and building trust that sustained the careers of generations of employees. Ultimately, the legacy of Garrett Freightlines has been carried on by its employees; the authors hope that this book preserves all that the employees accomplished even after they are gone. (Courtesy of Tyler Cantrell.)

Visit us at
arcadiapublishing.com

www.ingramcontent.com/pod-product-compliance
Lightning Source LLC
Chambersburg PA
CBHW050625110426
42813CB00007B/1717

9 781531 699048